AF584730

BY ROB FLOWER

ACKNOWLEDGEMENTS

I dedicate this book to my children and grandchildren with whom I wish to share my knowledge and memories, and to all those anglers out there who might find something within to encourage them in their pursuit of this gentle art.

I wish to acknowledge all the contributors to this collection, for without their willingness to share their information this book would not exist. Grateful thanks to Trevor Hawkins for his careful editing and some finer detail corrections regards flies and fly anglers. I also wish to thank Geraldine Martin and Alan Messina for correcting my woeful punctuation and some grammatical errors. Thanks also to my daughter Elizabeth for guiding me through my computer ignorance and helping with the layout. Thanks also to my publishers 'Australian Fishing Network' (AFN) Bill Classon and Debbie Sheldon-Collins for their encouragement to start the project. Gratitude is also due to Julian Patino, graphic art staff for his help with the layout. I also wish to thank my partner Rosemary for her help sorting out colours to compensate for my lack of colour discrimination.

Rob, my contribution to you wonderful collection. Trevor Hawkins

I would not dare to claim this is an original tie, it's basically a hares ear nymph. However, I first tied this pattern in the 1970's to use on cruising fish in backwaters, where I wanted a fly that would go straight through the surface film and then hang in the water with no movement and get still a look buggy enough for the fish to eat. It does this very well!

Hook Size 14 or 12 wide gape

Rib Heavy copper wire

Body Hares ear fur. To form a fat beetle shape

Hackle Two or three terns of brown hen hackle

Fish Inert!!. Set the Trap

Front cover flies;

Top left	Shiralee
Top right	Coachman
Centre left	Rosella fly
Centre right	Dragon fly
Bottom left	Zwar's Geehi Beetle
Centre	Shaving brush
Right	Hares ear nymph

Back cover flies from left to right

Left	Bomber boy
Middle	Black thing
Right	Watsons fancy

First published 2021

Published and distributed by
AFN Fishing & Outdoors
PO Box 544 Croydon, Victoria 3136
Telephone: (03) 9729 8788 Facsimile: (03) 9729 7833
Email: sales@afn.com.au
Website: www.afn.com.au

ISBN: 9781 865 13334 8

INTRODUCTION

Many of the flies herein are from anglers I have met and fished with. This compilation was started sometime in the 1980's and has continued spasmodically until the present day. I have tried to stick to the original materials and tying's and providing the names of the personalities who have shared their own patterns or their favourites. Those flies are supplemented by favourites and fancies from my own fly boxes. Some are directly from books as they looked fishy or buggy to me, while others are variants of flies I have seen and tied with the available materials I had at the time.

This book was original to be named The Rogues I have met and the flies they fish with, I came up with this catchy name only to attract interest. First up, let me say the reference to 'rogues' in no way should be taken as a reflection on the character of the contributors. Some are indeed great or colourful characters whatever that may mean, others are just patient, tolerant fishermen (nice people) and that seems to be the common requirement to pursue this gentle art. Without their kindness this collection would not exist.

Most of the patterns collected were handwritten and signed in an old blue lined exercise book.

I would have loved to publish these as they are, but the problems with scanning, removing lines and tidying up hundreds of drawings, (some a bit rough) were beyond me. I have described the flies with the background information I was given or personally know, and this comes with apologies for any unintended errors; no doubt there are many.

The flies may not be in strict order although the index may be of some help. I hope that searching through the flies will provide the reader with some exciting discoveries about how other angler's fish with favourite flies. Many of them have both wet and dry versions and I have included both where I thought appropriate.

I have claimed a very few flies as the originator, but that may not necessarily be true, if untrue, it is unintentional. They were original ideas for me at the time even though many others may have had the same inspiration before or since. In reality there is little possibility of making something entirely new. One of the odd things about flies is the name. Many names are used over and over, particularly those that sound catchy. Often a name can refer to a completely different fly. Anglers making flies that are new to them and searching for a name are often unaware the name can refer to other flies. It is also common to see flies almost the same as established patterns, but with a different name. It can be very confusing. The good thing about variants, is that mimicking something good is a form of flattery to the creator of the original. There must be millions of variant creations around the world, invented over hundreds of years by countless anglers, original? A few perhaps.

What fly will I fish with today? In making a selection, observation is a vital element, but experience tells me that fish are mostly required to eat the aquatic food available at the time. They also have to be opportunistic, but the food must come from the local food chain with a blend of seasonal terrestrials. A knowledge of the food chain is the bread and butter of success as it gives a number of alternatives to try and tempt a fish. My first book "*Australian Trout Food, Trout Flies and how to fish them*" describes the life cycle of the most common animals that fish see and eat. It also contains flies, and suggestions for fishing techniques. Flies that represent each of these food groups in different sizes and colours give the fly fisher a wide choice of things to try. Years of competition angling and experience tell me that if a technique or fly is not working "*try something different*". However, just continually changing flies is a mistake. Try as many techniques (like a wide variation of retrieves or sink times) as you can before tying on another fly. Something else that can work in still water is pulling a dry fly and making a wake with it. Try this when there is a hatch on, especially in breezy weather. A moving target attracts attention.

On English wet flies! Why they are not used more often I have no idea. They have survived for hundreds of years because they work. I use them a lot for the same reason.

One of my personal foibles is weighted flies. I always paint the heads of weighted flies with red nail polish to easily identify them from others in my box. Heavily weighted specimens are marked with a small black dot on the red varnish. Easy recognition of my weighted flies allows me to fish more of the vertical water column if I think the fish may be down deep. Unweighted flies with a normal retrieve would not get down more the 30cm and if fish are deeper, they simply will not come up to take a fly.

There are many references to loch style fishing throughout this book as I have done quite a lot of it over a number of years. This form of boat fishing often involves using a team of flies in a specified order. As the often 4.2 to 6 metre leader must roll out nicely, it is customary to put the heaviest fly at the end point and two others about 60-90cm apart above that. The order being something heavy (often larger) at the point, an insect replica on the middle dropper, and a bushier type fly or attractor at the top. The bushy fly is to create a wake when pulled across the water surface or left to hang there. The hang is often the most productive stage of retrieving flies. *Get the hang of it*. Fishing with three flies is not legal in some states even though it is the world standard. Special permits have to be obtained for major competitions where necessary. Three flies can also be very effective when nymph fishing in streams.

This example of a team of three comes from Ballarat angler Craig Coltman. Point fly "*yellow tailed stick fly*", middle dropper "*Connemara black*", and top dropper "*Kate McLaren*". Craig's notation is "*This is the team I fish on Lake Wendouree prior to Christmas on cool days. The common factor seems to be the yellow tails. I don't know why yellow works up to this time it just does. The team is fished on a 5m leader normally tied with 6lb Maxima treated with fuller's earth to make it sink. The team is fished with anything from a slow figure 8 retrieve right through to a fast rolly-polly.*"

The biggest leap in my angling experience was my introduction to competitive fly fishing through Fly Fish Australia. I was a member of North Suburban Fly Fishers' Club when an invitation to compete in the first ever Victorian Fly Fishers' Championships at Hamilton in Western Victoria in October 1993 attracted my interest.

Being a guide at the time and keen to compete, the club required potential representatives to compete in a weekend competition at the Lake Eildon Pondage. I duly tried out and though I caught enough fish, but because of my guiding experience I was appointed non-fishing Captain of the 'second best' team.

In due course we turned up to the venue at Lake Hamilton to be confronted with a small lake surround by a bicycle track of about 4km long. Annoyed at not fishing and being second best captain, I was determined that I should do everything necessary to improve our chances. Having walked the lake and knowing that I needed to spend time with and to encourage each of my team when they were fishing, I realised that it was not possible on foot. The road only covered one side of the lake and walking was too slow. Just then I noticed some boys on bikes going around the lake. Bright idea!! Hire a bike and ride around it. Not so easy on a weekend, so I persuaded one of the boys to hire me his bike for the day.

Armed with a map of the lake, I slowly went around it marking the map with every spot I saw a fish rise, knowing that fish will always stay close to the most prolific food sources. When the fishing started it was only a matter of knowing the beats my team had drawn and where in that 200 metre 'beat' I had seen a fish move. The rest is history as my team of mostly unknown anglers managed to win. It proved to me the value of knowing where the richest part of the food supply is to be found. The captain's gold medal is a prized possession.

If you ask a farmer which is his best paddock, he will always point out the one that has the richest piece of land. A lake is no different. The best piece of submerged land will always support the most livestock, in this case, water weed, aquatic insects and fish. Observation will tell you where the most swallows go to feed when insects are hatching. Problem solved.

I have since spent some years in competitive angling and it was a very steep learning curve. The best part was meeting the best anglers, learning from them, and sharing experiences. I have made many angling friends over the years, and as a result, many of them have contributed flies to this collection. I thank them one and all. After 60 years of fly fishing I am well aware of how little I actually know about fishing.

The memories this collection provoke are precious, and I hope they can be useful to other anglers. May you find inspiration in these pages to try something new or different?

CONTENTS

BEETLES

With over 30,000 species of beetles in Australia, there are plenty to choose from. Listed here are just a few of the popular patterns that many fly fishers use.

BLACK BEETLE 

For me this fly was born in the 1960's from the desire to create a less absorbent body and improve flotation.

Hook	#10-14
Tail	Black Hackle fibres
Wing case	Black crow strip
Body	Stiff dyed black cock hackle clipped short
Hackle	Ginger brown cock

BLACK TAG 

A variant on the red tag to imitate some of the small black beetles we frequently see. It works too. I have tried other colours as tags but they were not as good, even though they took the odd fish. The same fly with an orange tag is known as 'Treacle Parkin'.

Hook	#10-14
Tag	Black wool
Body	Bronze peacock herl
Hackle	Brown cock

CROCHETED CORIXIA 

Contributed by Barry Whelan of Ballarat.

Hook	#10-12
Underbody	Fine lead wire
Body top	Brown raffene
Underbody	White hi-viz
Legs	Brown goose biots
Head	Possum fur

FIERY BROWN BEETLE 

This fly has been around for ages and has proved itself many times over when brown beetles are about in early summer.

Hook	#10-12
Wing case	Brown hen
Body	Dubbed fiery brown seal fur
Rib	Fine gold or copper wire is optional
Hackle	Red/brown cock

GREAT LAKE BEETLE 

Credited to Malcom Gillies and Bill McCausland. Very definitely a Tasmanian fly, with wide acclaim.

Hook	#12
Body	Clipped black cock hackle
Wings	Dyed orange grizzle hackle x 2 angled back and clipped as illustrated
Hackle	Dyed orange grizzle cock

GUM BEETLE 

There are various species of these insects all over Australia, but for fly fishers the ones of interest are mostly Tasmanian. Some fly tiers put a small red spot at the butt of the foam back with a marker pen. The Tony Sloane pattern is easy to tie and effective. Just why these beetles are ignored on mainland Australia is a mystery as they are quite commonly seen in the bush.

Hook	#8-10
Body	Yellow thread.
Legs	Ginger cock hackle
Wingcase	White closed cell foam coloured yellow with permanent marker
Varnish	Clear nail polish, it also dissolves some plastics so if this happens try clear 'soft-dip'

JASSID 

Of unknown origin but certainly Tasmanian. Jassids are a Leaf Hopper species of cicada that occur in Tasmania in huge numbers every few years. Every Tasmanian and visiting fly angler look forward to a year of the Jassid.

Hook	#12
Wing case	Crow feather strip wide enough to double over
Body	Dyed red seals fur
Hackle	Small black cock

MCKENZIE BEETLE 

Believed to be a New Zealand tea-tree beetle imitation

Hook	#10-12
Tail	Peacock sword
Body	Bronze peacock herl
Wings	Peacock sword
Hackle	Black cock

MATCHAM'S JASSID

A beautifully tied fly originated by Laurie Matcham of Hobart, Tasmania.

Hook #12-14
Thread Black
Body Dubbed red antron
Wing White fluoro raffia coloured black but leaving a white strip on the trailing edge. Doubled over and tied in tent-like over the body
Hackle Black cock

MYSTERY BEETLE

Tier unknown. This fly is a mystery indeed as I have no idea where it came from, it was just there in my original pattern book after a number of contributors had written up their flies. I have fished it as a beetle and a snail with some good results. I suspect it may be the secret fly of a well-known Tasmanian guide.

Hook #14
Back Black raffia
Body Peacock herl tied plump
Legs Red crystal flash

PURPLE BEETLE

An original J.M.Gillies pattern tied by Lillian Miles and supplied by John Brooks

Hook #10-12
Back Black crow
Body Purple wool
Hackle Red brown cock

RED TAG

The favourite dry fly of so many Australian fly fishers. Its reputation as a fish catcher is legendary and it will tempt fish almost any time of the year. When tying the body of this fly, wrap the thread and the herl together as this helps to stop the herl from unwinding if a strand is broken. Round rather than thin bodies are most preferred. Too much hackle at the head can cause flies to spin and twist your leader. Origin is credited to a Worcestershire man named Flynn and the fly was first known as the 'Worcestershire Gem'. Strangely enough the Americans don't seem to fish this fly, and it doesn't appear in any of the North American fly pattern books I have. I wonder why?

Hook #8-18 most commonly 12-14
Tag Red wool or a pinkish looking colour of fluorescent red works well also
Body Bronze peacock herl. It can be palmered with stiff short hackle if preferred
Hackle Red or brown cock

BATTLESHIP RED TAG 

This fly was tied by Roger Butler from Hobart, a wise and experienced angler who runs Red Tag Fly Tours in Tasmania. It is an excellent indicator/attractor fly when used above bead heads or other sunken flies.

Hook	#10
Tail	Red wool
Body	Bronze peacock herl
Hackle	Light tan palmered. Tied in at tail and wound forward

RED TAG VARIANT 

This fly is from the late David Featherstone, a well-known Melbourne angler. Note the deer hair body designed to improve buoyancy.

Hook	#12-14
Tail	Red Ibis
Body	Clipped deer hair
Hackle	Ginger cock fully palmered

PARACHUTE RED TAG 

Tied as above but with a Hi-Viz post. I like and prefer this fly as it is easy to see and sits down well on the water.

Hook	#12-16
Tail	Red wool
Body	Peacock herl
Post	Hi-viz
Hackle	Brown tied parachute

RED ARSED BASTARD 

I have used this fly for many years, it may be from New Zealand, but I am unsure of that. This is the dry pattern used as a beetle. For some reason it works well on brown trout, they seem to be rather partial to red. There is also a longtail and wet fly version. I also tie it with red and brown hackle.

Hook	#10-14
Tail	Red floss
Butt	Red floss
Thorax	Peacock herl
Hackle	Black

ROYAL HUMPY

A Jack Dennis original that features in my pattern book, the inclusion is in his own handwriting and takes pride of place in my collection.

Hook	#10-14
Tail	Moose tail hair
Underbody	Dubbed fur or floss in yellow, red or other colours. Red being most common
Wingcase	Folded back grey deer hair
Hackle	Brown and grey grizzle mixed

SOLDIER BEETLE

Interesting little characters that can appear in great swarms in summer. The females lay eggs in the ground and the larvae are carnivorous, feeding on the eggs and larvae of other insects, especially grasshoppers.

Hook	#12-14 L/S
Body	Orange floss
Wingcase	Green raffia
Thorax	Black dubbing
Hackle	Dyed green cock

TROTHODG

Generally accredited to Tasmanian Dick Trotter, this is a general beetle fly with all the necessary elements. It works equally well with red or brown hackle.

Hook	#12-14
Tail	Nil
Body	Peacock herl
Legs	Golden pheasant tippets on either side sloping back
Centre	Black cock hackle
Thorax	Peacock herl
Hackle	Black cock

TEA TREE BEETLE

An old Tasmanian version, which is where this pattern probably originated.

Hook	#12-14
Wing Case	Strip of brown hen quill feather wide enough to double over
Body	Black Ostrich herl
Hackle	Short black cock

WATER BEETLE

Hook #10-12
Back Slips of brown turkey
Body Yellow or light brown wool
Legs Red biots tied in halfway along the body

WET BLACK BEETLE

I have found this fly successful in the colder months when terrestrials are scarce, and fish are hungry. When thoroughly wet it will sink slowly and can be left sinking for quite a time. A take will be indicated by a tightening of the line.

Hook #10-12
Body Black coarse knitting wool
Wings Black crow
Hackle Black hen

WESTERN LAKES BEETLE

Simon Taylor of Devonport, Tasmania, uses this conspicuous fly for polaroiding in the Western Highlands of Tasmania.

Hook #10-14
Tail Lime green yarn with pearl flashabou
Body Palmered black cock trimmed to the width of the hook gape
Hackle Black

ZWAR'S GEEHI BEETLE

The original of this well-known fly was created by Dr Keith Zwar of Melbourne. He was a WW1 Doctor from a very distinguished Melbourne family. The Geehi, as it is most commonly known, is an excellent searching pattern for streams, and I, no doubt along with many others have caught many fish on it.

Hook #12-16
Tail Golden pheasant tippet
Body Peacock herl palmered with ginger cock hackle
Hackle A darker ginger cock

CADDIS

Australia has around 600 known species of caddis and there are a wide variety of flies to imitate many of them.

ANDORRAN CADDIS

This fly came from Adellach Rincon, who represented Andorra at one of the World Fly-fishing Championships.

Hook	#12-14
Tail	Cock de Leon
Body	Muskrat dubbing
Wing	Cock de Leon Hackle Points
Hackle	Cock de Leon (one turn only)

CADDIS

Contributed by Coato Rerling during the 1996 World Fly-fishing Championships. It represents a spent caddis. The body colour can be varied to suit local species.

Hook	#12-14
Body	Sparse yellow dubbing
Wing	CDC

CADDIS EMERGER

One of my own variants.

Hook	#12
Underbody	Fine lead wire
Body	Hares' ear fur
Rib	Fine gold wire
Hackle	Brown partridge
Head	Red varnish

CDC EMERGER

Hook	#12-14
Tail	Short tag of fluoro green wool
Body	Cream wool or superfine dubbing
Rib	Fine gold wire
Wing	Fawn or grey CDC feathers
Legs	Brown partridge
Head	Hare's ear dubbing

CROCHETED CADDIS PUPA

This pattern was the contribution of Torril Kolbu in 1996. She has been a world champion fly tier in the past, is a professional tier and originator of the most exquisite flies and is credited with inventing crocheted bodies on flies.

Hook	Mustad Caddis bend #10-12
Weight	Lead wire
Body	Crocheted from different coloured antron yarn
Wing Case	Slips from a duck wing feather
Legs	Partridge hackle
Antennae	Bronze mallard
Thorax	Dubbed dark grey fox

CREEL CADDIS

From Bruce Smith, a trout guide from Central Victoria. Tied to imitate the fluttering adult stage of the snowflake caddis.

Hook	#14-16
Body	Thinly dubbed common rabbit underfur
Rib	Fine gold wire
Body hackle	Very small pale Cree or ginger grizzle, palmered
Wings	Pale quail feathers
Hackle	Cree to match body

DARK PEEKING CADDIS

Hook	#12-16
Body	Dark dubbed hare's ear
Rib	Fine copper wire
Hackle	Dark quail rump
Head	Black ostrich herl

DIVING CADDIS

It is the habit of many female caddis to re-enter the water to lay eggs after mating. This is a Gary La Fontaine pattern.

Hook	#12-14
Body	Tan dubbing
Wing	Clear Antron over brown partridge fibres
Hackle	One turn of sparse small brown hen

EMERGENT CADDIS

Origin unknown.

Hook	#12 caddis bend
Body	Light green sparkle dubbing
Wings	Snipe tied as stubs at the sides
Hackle	Brown partridge

EMERGENT SPARKLE CADDIS PUPA

This pattern was provided by legendary USA fly guru Gary La Fontaine during a visit to Australia. His extensive knowledge of caddis is well illustrated in his book 'Caddis Flies', and several of his other books. This fly mimics an emerging pupa in its translucent bubble rising to the surface.

Hook	#12-14
Body	Dubbed sparkle yarn
Wing	Deer hair
Head	Superfine dubbing

GOULBURN CADDIS

An excellent free-swimming larvae pattern by the late Murray 'MUZ' Wilson.

Hook	#12-14 caddis bend
Underbody	Lead wire
Body	Dubbed green blend of seal fur
Rib	Copper wire
Thorax	Peacock herl
Head	Red varnish

GREEN PETER

An excellent Irish fly for emerging caddis. I caught a trout of 3 kg on this fly one November from East Moorabool Reservoir. I have caught many others since by using it as a single fly while fishing from a boat, also in springtime. My special way of fishing it is with what I call a dibbly-dabbly retrieve. Casting the unweighted fly on about 6m of fly-line plus the leader, I allow about a 5 second sink time, then slowly lift the rod while gently shaking it and literally making the fly dance in the water. When the fly gets close, I roll cast it out again at an angle of 15 degrees from the previous one. By continually changing the angles of every cast, each cast is to new water as the boat drifts along. Try it, it is tiring but it works.

Hook	#10-12
Tail	None
Body	Light green seal fur
Palmer	Ginger cock
Rib	Fine gold wire
Wing	Hen Pheasant
Hackle	Ginger

GREENWELL'S GLORY 

A traditional English wet fly that has claimed a great many fish for me and is one of my 'go to' flies for river fishing. The brainchild of Cannon William Greenwell of Durham, it is likely the most famous fly of them all along with the Royal Coachman. It is a good imitation for emerging caddis.

Hook	#12-14
Tail	Nil
Body	Well waxed yellow thread
Rib	Fine gold wire
Wings	Duck wing slips
Hackle	Cochybondhu

GREEN TAG STICK 

The contribution of Chris Ogborne, English fly-fishing team captain in 1996. He regards it as a top fly on some of the best lakes in the world.

Hook	#10
Tag	Fluoro green wool
Body	Natural peacock herl
Rib	Fine copper wire
Hackle	Hen badger tied sparse

GREY DUSTER 

A pattern I found in FADG Griffiths book 'The Lure of Fly Fishing'. However, the originator of the fly is unknown. I have met many anglers who like and use this simple fly with good success.

Hook	#12-16
Thread	Grey
Tail	Grizzle cock
Body	Dubbed rabbit underfur
Hackle	Grizzle

GRAYLING CADDIS 

Adam Royter supplied this simple to tie fly that works.

Hook	#14-18 fine wire
Body	Fine caddis green dubbing, dubbed around the bend
Wing	Tan CDC with deer hair on top

HYDROPSYCHE CADDIS LARVAE

These flies are from Englishman Oliver Edwards during the 1996 world championships. Oliver ties the most exquisite flies and is a regular contributor to English fly-fishing magazines. This pattern represents a free-swimming caddis larvae.

Hook	Partridge K4A #8-14 (or a caddis bend if not available)
Tail	Soft filoplume
Abdomen	Masterclass 4 ply yarn lightly teased out (or substitute)
Carapace	Flexi body or latex
Legs	Golden pheasant fibres

HYDROPSYCHE CADDIS LARVAE

These two patterns are also free swimmers from Geoff Clarkson, a former captain of English fly-fishing teams. Pictures of the flies are herewith. Geoff did not specify the materials but if tied from similar materials to Oliver Edward's flies a good result will be achieved. This larvae can vary widely in colour, but pale olives and browns predominate.

Hook	Caddis bend 8-14
Thread	To match
Abdomen	Wool yarn (fine)
Back	Brown turkey or similar
Rib	Fine silver wire
Tail	Filo plume
Legs	Small hen hackle

IRRESISTIBLE CADDIS PUPA

Hook	#10-14 caddis bend
Thread	Red
Butt	Fluoro green dubbing
Body	Three translucent glass beads
Thorax	Hares ear with protruding guard hairs
Head	Gold bead

JAYS DUN CADDIS

A fly supplied by Jay Buckner, skipper of a number of USA world fly fishing teams. A fly that he said fishes well on evening rises to spent caddis. Note: There are many Australian small dark caddis that would be well imitated by a #16-18 version of this fly.

Hook	#12
Body	A few strands of dark grey goose quill
Wings	Two strips darkest duck quill tied tent like over body and coated with flex cement
Antennae	Two fine stripped hackle points
Hackle	Four or five turns of dark dun, trimmed flat on top

LEAD WING COACHMAN (VARIANT) WET

A good emergent caddis fly that I like to fish straight across stream.

Hook	#10-12
Tail	Golden Pheasant tippets
Butt	Peacock herl
Waist	Red floss
Thorax	Peacock herl
Wing	Grey wing slips
Hackle	Brown hen

LEADHEAD NYMPH

A deepwater fly for fast flowing streams and fished like a bead head. The invention of Hans Van Klinken, best known for his famous 'Klinkhammer Special' dry fly. This is a fly I have fished to replicate free swimming caddis larvae.

Hook	#8-14
Butt	Fluoro lime green wool
Hackle	Brown partridge in front of the butt
Body	Brown rabbit dubbed in a dubbing loop
Head	A lead split shot. Crimped on 3kg mono and tied by both ends with the split facing the eye

LITTLE BLACK CADDIS

These are fairly common insects, and trout take them readily.

Hook	#14-18
Body	Any fine black dubbing applied sparsely
Post	White Hi-Viz
Hackle	Black cock tied parachute fashion

MONARO CADDIS

Supplied by "Kay" Kaj 'Bushy' Busch, who resides in Pambula and fishes the Snowy Mountains, especially Lake Eucumbene. About 20 years ago I was fishing alone on Lake Jindabyne and this deep voice took me by surprise. "Bushy" had walked a considerable distance not to fish but just to say "Hello". Always helpful and freely giving of his vast knowledge, altogether a great bloke.

Hook	#16
Body	Dubbed fluff from the base of a cock pheasant green rump feather
Wing	Cock pheasant rump feather
Hackle	Brown cock

ORANGE CADDIS

Jan Spencer, fly tier to Australian flyfishing teams including the winning Australian team at Jindabyne in 2000. It should be noted that orange is a colour common in many species of caddis.

Hook	#12-14
Thread	Black
Body	Orange floss
Wing	Grey cock tied as a wonder wing
Hackle	Black, clipped on top
Head	Black thread wound through the hackle.
	Note: the wonder wing was invented by the late G.E.P. "George" Rowney, 'Old Mudguts' of the Southern Fly fishers Association

REESY'S CADDIS

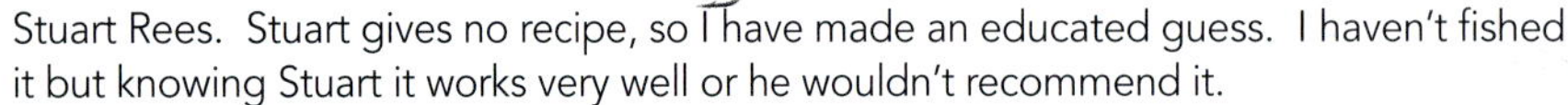

Stuart Rees. Stuart gives no recipe, so I have made an educated guess. I haven't fished it but knowing Stuart it works very well or he wouldn't recommend it.

Hook	#12-14
Body	Dubbed light brown fur
Wing	Light coloured deer hair
Hackle	White

ROB'S EASY SEE CADDIS

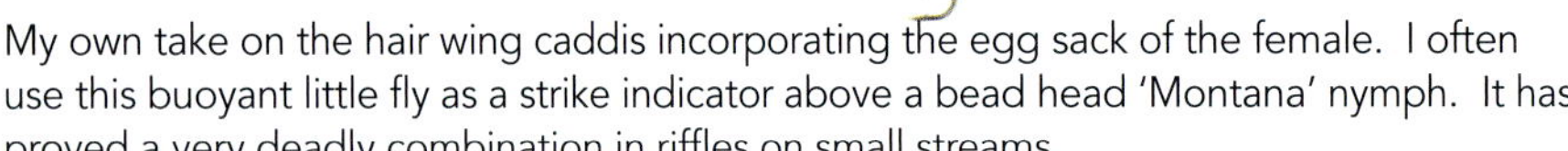

My own take on the hair wing caddis incorporating the egg sack of the female. I often use this buoyant little fly as a strike indicator above a bead head 'Montana' nymph. It has proved a very deadly combination in riffles on small streams.

Hook	#14
Butt	One turn of fluoro green wool
Body	Blended seal fur 50% light green, 30% light brown, 10% natural, 10% yellow
Palmer	Short brown cock hackle
Rib	Fine gold wire
Wing	Fairly thick bunch of white deer hair

ROD'S SNOWFLAKE CADDIS

Another successful fly from Rod Barford, trout and hunting guide extraordinaire.

Hook	#12-14
Body	Dubbed grey antron
Wing	Folded white gift wrap ribbon
Hackle	White cock trimmed at the bottom

SEDGE

Sedge is the common name for caddis in the UK and parts of Europe.

Hook	#10-12
Tail	Red hackle fibres
Body	Honey coloured dubbing
Wings	Light grey duck or similar
Hackle	Light ginger, fully palmered

ROYAL COACHMAN WET VERSION

A very famous fly indeed and a personal favourite. American's claim it was invented by an American John Haily in 1878, but the English claim it also. This fly has justified its world-wide fame. I use this fly also as a wet when snowflake caddis are hatching, casting and retrieving straight across the current. Variants have a different colour waist of orange, yellow or grey. All are successful.

Hook	#8-14
Tail	Golden Pheasant tippets
Butt	Peacock herl
Waist	Red floss
Thorax	Peacock herl
Wing	White duck quill slips
Hackle	Brown hen

SKATING CADDIS

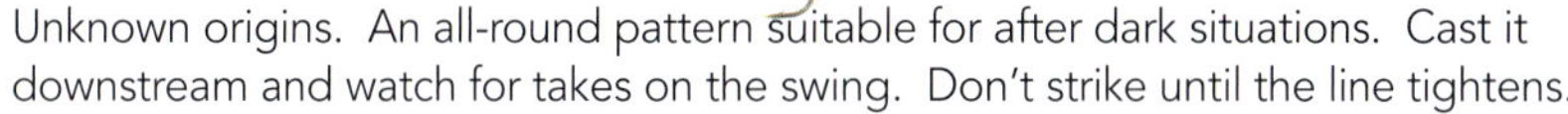

Unknown origins. An all-round pattern suitable for after dark situations. Cast it downstream and watch for takes on the swing. Don't strike until the line tightens.

Hook	#12-14 Caddis bend
Body	Fur from a hare's ear
Wing	CDC feathers
Collar	Olive deer hair
Head	Hare's ear fur

SHANNON MOTH

An original pattern from one of Australia's most respected fly fishers, Dick Wigram. His books, the "The Shannon Rise" and "Nymph Fishing in the Southern Hemisphere" are part of our fly-fishing folklore and worth a lot of dollars to collectors, as are his other books. The pattern is from Max Stokes "Tasmanian Trout Fly Patterns". The fly itself represents Asmicridae Grisea.

Male:

Hook	#12 up-eye
Body	Cream and blue/grey fur mixed and lightly dubbed on
Wing	Strip of grey duck wing quill and a strip of barred teal breast feather

SHANNON MOTH CONT...

Female:

Hook	#12
Body	Fawn fur lightly dubbed on.
Wings	Strip of brown mallard shoulder feather
Hackle	Brown partridge clipped short Short grizzle hackle can also be used
Note	These flies were sometimes tied end to end to imitate a copulating pair

SNOWFLAKE CADDIS

The snowflake caddis found on the Australian mainland is Asmicridae Edwardsii and almost identical to the Tasmanian species Asmicridae Grisea. I tie it to match this common snowflake caddis, but I make no claims as its originator, for it is only a variant on so many other similar flies.

Hook	#12-14
Tail	Grizzle hackle (caddis don't have tails but it helps with flotation)
Body	School grey wool
Wing	White duck quill tied flat and cut to match body length
Hackle	Grizzle

SNOWFLAKE CADDIS

Origin unknown.

Hook	#12-14
Tail	White hackle tips
Body	Cream dubbing palmered with very small white hackle
Rib	Fine gold wire
Wing	White deer hair with crystal flash
Hackle	Grizzle

STICK CADDIS NYMPH

The late Murray 'MUZ' Wilson tied the first of these that I'm aware of for fishing in the Camperdown Lakes of 'Bullen Merri' and 'Purrumbete'. It is a very realistic fly and does the job. Let it sink deep and retrieve it with a slow figure 8 retrieve.

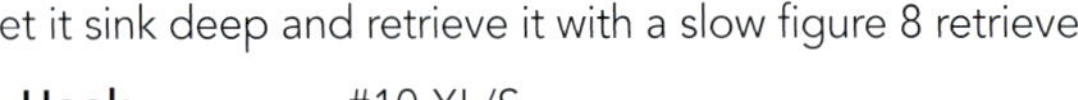

Hook	#10 XL/S
Body	Singed brown synthetic dubbing
Head	Singed yellow antron yarn

STICK CADDIS NYMPH

Nothing new about this one, it has been around for ages.

Hook	#12 L/S
Body	Several strands of cock pheasant centre tail
Rib	Fine gold wire
Head	Yellow or cream floss
Hackle	Two turns only of very small ginger or cree

STIMULATOR

Originally invented by famous American angler and fly innovator Randall Kaufmann. Another fly with a lot of variants. The original seems to have had a palmered olive body, others have orange and yet another has the same body as a fully palmered royal coachman. In Australia a yellow or orange body seems most popular.

Hook	TMC200R #6-16
Tail	Grey deer hair
Body	Olive "Hairtron' dubbing
Palmer	Brown hackle
Rib	Fine gold wire wound counterclockwise to the hackle
Wing	Grey deer hair
Head	Amber dubbing
Hackle	Grizzle wound over the head

STIMULATOR

This one comes from Rick Dobson of Aussie Angler fame and is a favoured summer small stream fly or as a strike indicator.

Hook	#10
Tail	Deer hair
Body	Peacock herl, palmered with brown hackle
Wing	Deer hair with an over-wing of white hi-viz
Legs	Black & white barred rubber
Hackle	Mixed grizzle and brown

TEAL AND RED

Another of those old English wet patterns that is a successful imitation of emerging caddis in lakes.

Hook	#12
Tail	Golden Pheasant tippets
Body	Red wool
Rib	Silver oval tinsel
Wing	Rolled teal or barred wood duck breast feather
Hackle	Ginger hen

THE FREEK

From Freek Slomp, a member of the Dutch world fly-fishing team.

Hook	#12
Tail	Golden Pheasant tippets
Body	Dubbed Muskrat fur
Wing	2 CDC feathers
Hackle	Ginger brown

WHITE CDC CADDIS

It floats really well.

Hook	#12-16
Body	Dubbed white CDC
Wing	Three white CDC feathers
Thorax	Dubbed white CDC

WHITE BEAD HEAD

This remarkable accidental discovery happened at Hepburn Lagoon, Victoria. I had landed a rainbow of about 1kg and when removing my 'Winter Blue' midge larvae from its jaw I saw this white bead head with a short length of leader attached. Obviously broken off. The fly will have another name but who knows what it may be?

Hook	#10
Tail	Red wool 4mm long and two strands of crystal-flash about 12mm
Body	Mixed colour mostly black ice chenille
Head	4mm pearly white glass bead

WHITE MOTH

An imitation of the snowflake caddis that is favoured by many anglers.

Hook	#12-14
Tail	White hackle
Body	White floss
Wings	Strips of white duck quill
Hackle	White cock

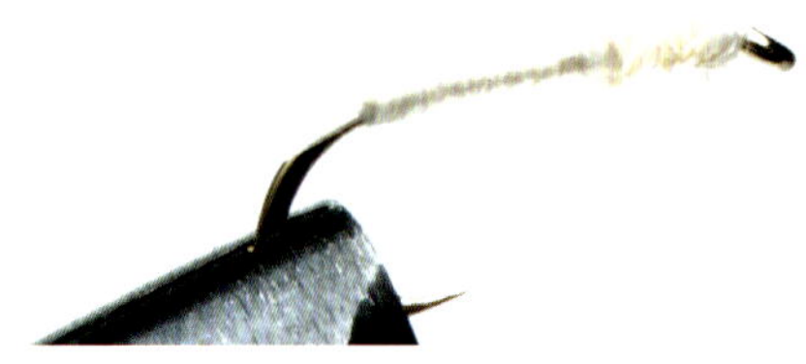

WHITE WULFF

The 'Wulff' series of flies were all developed by American Lee Wulff and there are numerous variants. As far as I'm aware this is the original but there are others as well that are all white.

Hook	#10-14
Tail	White calf tail
Body	Cream fur dubbing
Wings	White calf upright and split
Hackle	Very light badger

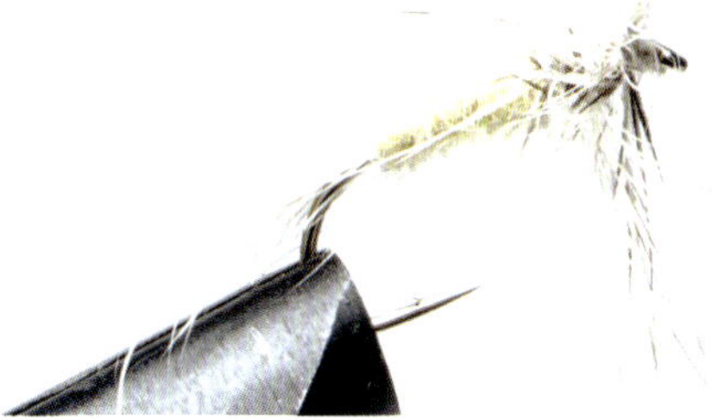

CHIRONOMID/MIDGES

Midges occur in massive numbers and the larvae can, in ideal conditions, reach 100,000 to the square metre of mud bottom. Commonly the larvae are blood red, about as thick as a pin and 12-15mm long. Bloodworm flies are literally left to hang in the water. The line will draw if the fly is taken by a fish.

The best exponents of midge fishing I know are Norm King and 'The Senator', Shane Murphy. The expertise of this pair chasing big fish feeding on midges is legendary. Accuracy of casting, reading the direction of fish and speed of presentation of the fly being the crucial elements. Fishing for trout taking midge from the surface, often in slicks or wind lanes is for me a very exciting prospect, the important factor for success is to place the fly in the path of a rising fish. Learn to fish midges, its success will stun you if you take the time to develop your skills. England might be considered the home of Midge and Buzzer fishing.

Geoff Clarkson eight times captain of English fly-fishing teams provided pupa and emerger patterns for general use. They would be equally useful in Australian conditions.

Geoff patterns include Diawl Bach, Black Midge pupa, Hares ear nymph, Pheasant tail nymph, and Red Midge pupa.

BALLING MIDGE

There are other colours for this fly although only the grey one is shown here. Extra-long hackle may be clipped on a black version, but I prefer mine to be about 1½ times the width of the gape. Balling midge phenomena, though infrequent creates an exciting feeding frenzy that may last from a few minutes to half an hour. I am yet to see one that has exceeded that. Fast accurate casting is the key to success.

Hook	#12-14
Hackle	Badger, heavily palmered

BLOODWORM

Hook	Mustad wide gape #8-12
Body	Blood red tying thread
Rib	Black thread
Hackle	One turn of black hen

BLACK EMERGER

Hook #12-16 caddis bend
Body Sparse black dubbing
Wing stubs Dark grizzle hackle points
Thorax Black dubbing

BLACK MIDGE

Supplied by Andrew Overton, best known as a tyer of superb full dressed salmon flies.

Hook #22-24
Tail Three black hackle fibres
Body Black tying thread
Wings White 'Hi-Viz'

BLACK MIDGE PUPA

Hook #10-14 Caddis bend
Body Black floss, varnished with clear nail polish
Rib Fine copper wire
Wing Cases Orange feather slips on either side of the thorax
Thorax Black dubbing lightly teased out

BLARNEY MIDGE

A Pat O'Keefe pattern from the Lake Taupo area of New Zealand. As is usual for Pat, this is a simple but effective fly.

Hook #14-16
Body Sparsely dubbed seal fur teased out
Wing Stubs Clipped white duck quill slips

BOB'S BITS

An English fly that can be a midge pupa, a caddis or a nymph. It was designed by Bob Worts for use on his home territory of Graffam Water in the UK. It is easy to tie, simple fare, and that might be why it is so effective.

Hook	#10-14
Body	Olive seals fur
Rib	Pearl Mylar
Wing	White goose or swan wing fibre
Hackle	Furnace hen

CDC SUSPENDER

Hook	#14-20
Tail	Sparse strands of 'Hi-Viz'
Body	Dubbed fur to suit
Wingcase	CDC
Thorax	Dubbed darker fur
Wing	CDC pulled over thorax shuttle cock style

CHIRONOMID EMERGER

I obtained this pattern from a South African I met in 2000. This is a fly I have used a lot in winter with some success.

Hook	#12-14
Tail	4 black hackle fibres tied short
Body	Fine black dubbing
Rib	Fine blue Lurex fibres
Wing Case	Blue Lurex

CHIRONOMID NYMPH

Two more John Rumpf flies.

Hook	#12-14
Body	Stripped peacock herl dyed black with marker pen
Thorax	Peacock herl from sword feather
Breathers	White hi-viz

STYLE 2

Hook	#12-14
Tag	White hi-viz cut short
Body	Black sparkle dub mixed with black rabbit guard hairs that are then clipped
Head	Black tying thread

COPPER JOHN

In sizes 14-16 this is an excellent midge larvae imitation. See the entry under 'NYMPHS' for tying details.

Hook	#10-18 X/l or XX/L
Tail	Goose biots
Underbody	Lead wire to about mid-shank then over-bound with thread to from an
even	taper
Body	Copper wire tapered up to the thorax
Legs	Hen hackle
Thorax	Peacock herl
Wingcase	"Thin skin" or dark turkey with a strip of holographic tinsel over the top
	After completion a coat of epoxy is applied to the wing case. It may need two coats if turkey is used as the first will soak in

DIAWL BACH

A Welsh fly supplied by that doyen of Welsh fly fishing and BBC presenter Moc Morgan. His son Hywell is equally well known as a world champion fly caster. The fly is credited to a Mr Evans of Cardiff.

I have used this as a dropper fly above a "Bugger Me" for lake fishing from the shore in winter. Its best capture so far is a brownie of almost 3kg.

Hook	#12-14. I use a 14
Tail	Brown hackle fibres
Body	Very thin peacock herl
Hackle	Two only turns of brown hen

FORE AND AFT

Another example of ingenuity that works when midges are balling on the surface

Hook	#14-16
Rear hackle	Blue dun with shiny side forward
Body	Dubbed muskrat underfur
Hackle	Blue dun with shiny side facing backward

GARRETT'S BLACK AND ORANGE

A fly recommended by old friend Jason Garret, formerly of London Lakes in Tasmania. Jason has tripped up many a fine fish on this little fly when they wouldn't look at anything else.

Hook	#16
Tail	Black cock hackle fibres
Body	Orange silk
Hackle	Black cock

GREEN MIDGE EMERGER

Hook	#14-18 caddis bend
Tail	Crystal Flash to represent a 'cast off' shuck
Body	Stripped peacock herl
Thorax	Lime green dubbing
Breathers	White Hi-Viz

GREEN MIDGE

A very common fly, and an important food item, not because of its size, but because of its vast numbers!!

Fish dead drift on a floating line.

Hook	#16-20
Tail	Crystal Flash
Body	Stripped peacock herl
Thorax	Lime green dubbing
Breather's	Hi-Viz

GREEN PALMER

Jon Lindsey, an England world team member uses this variant of the 'soldier palmer fly" as a top dropper when there are green midge on the water.

Hook	#10-14
Tail	A few fibres of the body material pricked out
Body	Dubbed olive seal fur
Rib	Fine gold wire
Hackle	Palmered natural red

GREY EMERGER

A fly of unknown origin that I tied for myself and have shared with some friends. In the mid 1990's I gave a couple to John Sautelle Jr whose comment was "*I fished with this fly in the Victorian championships in 1995. In the morning 3 hour session of the second day it took 6 fish making a large contribution to my winning the competition. It now holds a permanent place in my fly box. Thanks Rob*".

Hook	#14
Body	Stripped peacock herl
Wings	Grizzle hackle points
Thorax	Dubbed grey mink

HARES EAR NYMPH

Hook	#12-14
Tail	Brown hackle fibres
Body	Dubbed hares ear fur
Rib	Fine copper wire
Thorax	Hare's ear fur

MASSIES MIDGE

Rick Massie

Hook	#16-18
Back	Polar Flash
Body	Green dubbing
Rib	Fine gold wire
Head	Sparse orange dubbing

MIDGE PUPA

Contributed by Geoff Naylor, who fishes extensively in Southern NSW, where he lives. He notes that the black and silver rib makes the orange darker and is the same as the natural ascending pupa.

Hook	#12-16 caddis bend
Tail	Black hackle
Body	Rear ½ orange floss front ½ black seal fur picked out
Rib	Black thread and silver wire
Wing case	Crow

MINK EMERGER

This fly is especially good in the margins at Lake Eucumbene when the water level is high, and the fish are in shallow water. It is fished with an ultra-slow figure 8 retrieve. I have seen it catch fish with phenomenal success and it is so simple to tie.

Hook	#14-16
Body	Pinkish mink fur tied sparsely with guard hairs picked out

PHEASANT TAIL NYMPH

First tied by famous english riverkeeper Frank Sawyers circa 1930.

Hook	#14-16
Underbody	Copper wire
Tail	Pheasant tail fibres
Body	Wrapped Pheasant tail fibres
Rib	Fine copper wire
Wing case	Pheasant tail fibres

PURVEY'S PUPA

Developed by retired Victorian guide Alistair Purvey and used mostly in the Ballarat area.

The fly is best fished on a greased leader and left static where and when fish are rising to midge. Other colours would also be effective.

Hook	#18 dry fly
Body	Green tinsel overwound with olive thread
Thorax	Black seal fur

REED SMUT

An English pattern I have found effective on small streams.

Hook	#16-20
Butt	Silver oval tinsel
Middle	Peacock sword herl
Head	Silver tinsel

RICK'S MIDGE

Supplied by Rick Massie, who fishes it with a very slow 'figure 8' retrieve, or casts it to a moving fish and slowly lifts the rod. He has had success with it in Eucumbene, Jindabyne and lakes around Ballarat. He advises to grease the leader to within 20cm of the fly.

Hook #12-18
Body Green olive Antron
Rib Four turns of copper wire
Back Strip of holographic Mylar
Thorax Hot orange dubbing

RED MIDGE PUPA

Hook #12 caddis bend
Body Red thinly dressed seal fur
Rib Fine copper wire
Thorax Peacock herl

ROD'S MIDGE PUPA

From Rod Barford, a professional guide who runs "Fly Trek".

Hook #14 Kamasan B100
Thread Black
Tail Short sparse fluoro white wool
Body Stripped peacock herl
Thorax Light grey antron dubbing
Breather's Short sparse fluoro white wool

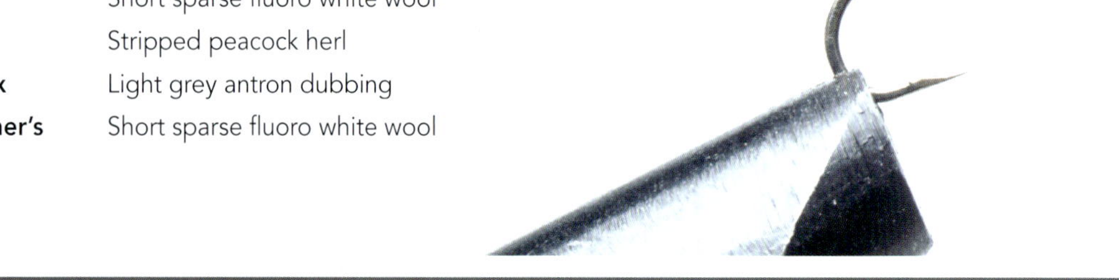

SIMPLE MIDGE PUPA

This fly has achieved great success during the winter months in Tasmania. Unweighted, it is fished dead drift on a floating line and has caught some very large fish in Blackman's Lagoon. It is a very easy fly to tie. Simply lash a length of white Hi-Viz to the hook shank and trim the ends short.

Hook #12-14
Tail White Hi-Viz
Body Black thread

SUSPENDER PUPA

In the hatching process, pupa rise to the water surface and hang suspended for a short time. Some pupa, however, are unable to hatch and get stuck in the meniscus, where they are mopped up by cruising fish. This fly was originally the work of American nymphing legend Charles E Brooks whose book 'Nymph Fishing for Larger Trout' is a great insight into how fish feed in fast water.

Hook	#12-14 caddis bend
Tail	A few strands of white Hi-Viz
Body	Sparse black or other colour seal fur
Rib	Fine silver wire
Wing-case	Orange feather slips
Thorax	Thin dark peacock herl
Head	Polystyrene bead or closed cell foam

WINTER BLUE

A fly I have had success with at various lakes in the colder months. Lead wire is an option for deep water. There are two versions, with and without a glass bead. The fly is a variant of Ken Orr's 007.

Hook	#12-14 Caddis bend
Tail	Black cock hackle
Body	Black floss
Rib	Narrow silver or wire
Thorax	Blue Sparkle Dub
Bead	Blue glass bead is optional

DAMSELS AND DRAGON FLIES

ASSAM DRAGON

A mudeye pattern from Charles Brooks author of Nymph Fishing for Larger Trout. This book is an excellent read for 'upstream nymph' fishing enthusiasts. Heavily weighted flies for fishing in rough water on larger streams.

Hook	#6-8 L/S
Tail	None
Body	Wrapped brown seal fur or muskrat on the skin cut 3mm wide on the cross
Hackle	Brown dyed Grizzle

BLACK MUDDLER MINNOW

This is as effective as any of the other flies for night-time, during mudeye hatches. Also a good black cricket imitation.

Hook	#6-10
Tail	Black squirrel
Body	Silver tinsel
Wing	Black crow
Head	Dyed black deer hair

BLARNEY DAMSEL

Pat O'Keefe, famed New Zealand angler, guide and Blarney Lodge owner provided this damsel pattern for me in 2003. This is a very simple but effective fly.

Hook	#10
Tail	Green Rabbit fur
Body	Dubbed green rabbit teased out

CUBIT'S MUDEYE

A floating fly for night-time fishing. The aim is to 'chug' the fly across the surface film leaving a wake. I met the designer of this fly nearly thirty years ago at Lake Toolondo where he was waiting for night to come. Invented by Simon Gubit in Tasmania.

Hook	#8-10
Body	Preformed beige rubber that is colour brown on top with a marker
Legs	Deer hair strands left uncut from the head
Head	Spun deer hair

DAMSEL NYMPH

John Rumpf. John extensively fishes damsel nymphs slow and deep.

Hook	#12 L/S
Tail	Dyed green Partridge
Body	Mixture of green, peacock, and rainbow Laser-Dub
Rib	Copper wire
Eyes	Nylon beads
Wing case	Cock pheasant centre tail

DAMSEL NYMPH

Mick first tied this fly in about 1992/3. His use of 1cm of nylon before tying in the tail is to prevent the tail from wrapping around the hook which is very annoying. This innovation should be applied to all flies with long marabou tails, including woolly buggers and matuka's. His advice is to fish the fly slowly with 6-10cm strips with the rod tip down on the water surface.

Hook #14 L/S
Tail 12mm 6lb nylon to prevent the tail twisting around the hook
Tail Bunch of olive marabou tied long
Body Dubbed olive marabou feathers
Thorax Dyed olive rabbit
Eyes Small olive glass beads on burnt nylon

DAMSEL FLY

I found this fly in the very old fishing diary of Eric Harrison, a long since deceased veteran angler from "Auterdoo" near Bombala in New South Wales.

Hook #12 XXL
Tail Blue parrot tail feathers or blue macaw
Body Blue dyed condor or substitute
Rib Fine gold wire
Hackle Mixed badger and blue dun

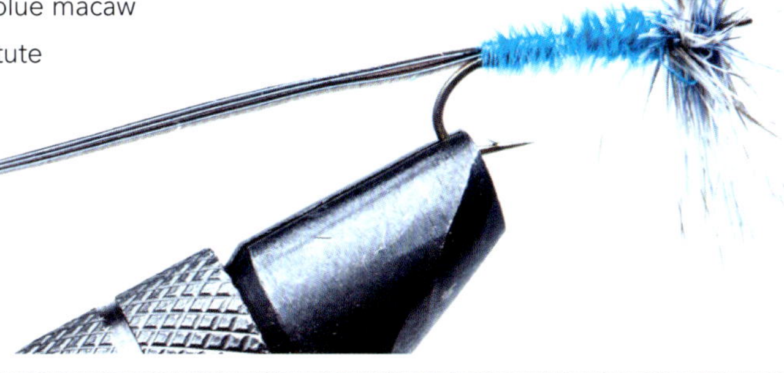

DAMSEL FLY (RESTING)

My own variant to imitate female blue damsels that land on the water prior to submerging and laying their eggs.

Tail Braided nylon marked blue with black bars
Thorax Blue floss silk
Wing 2 pale grizzle hackle feathers, back to back
Hackle Grizzle cock
Eyes Nylon stopper or 'burned' nylon

DRAGON FLY

This is Woodard's original pattern as published by David Scholes in *"Ripples Runs and Rises"*.

Hook XL/S 4 or 6
Tail 2 dyed green grizzle hackles back to back
Body Peacock herl, palmered with short dyed olive-green grizzle
Rib Very narrow yellow floss
Hackle Dyed red first, with dark blue at the front

MAGOO

Vern Barby, a well-known Ballarat angler and many times Australian competitor at world fly championships came up with this fly which is like a scaled down version of a woolly bugger. The fly is named after Vern's old fishing mate Alan 'Magoo' Howard. It has earned him many points of gratitude from those who use his famous fly. I understand it came about to imitate damsel fly larvae in Lake Wendouree, it is the green version that is best known but also works in brown. It was originally fished with a very slow retrieve but now Vern fishes it much faster. I have heard it many times and found myself saying it too "aaahhh Magoo you've done it again". There are quite a number of variants. *'Congrats Vern on a great fly'*.

Hook	#14
Tail	Marabou
Body	Dubbed marabou ribbed with fine copper wire
Eyes	Clear or burnt nylon
Hackle	One turn of soft dyed grizzle

MID AIR MAGICIAN

This is a blue damsel imitation from Roger Butler of Red Tag Tours in Hobart. He modified the pattern to tempt fish chasing damsel flies that often prove very frustrating. It was adapted from Woodard's dragon fly.

Hook	#8 L/S
Tail	Died blue hackle feather
Body	Sparse peacock herl
Rib	A single strand stripped from yellow floss
Palmer	Blue hackle
Hackle	One each of blue, ginger and olive

RUMPH'S DAMSEL NYMPH

John Rumph has caught some marvellous fish on this fly by fishing it slow and deep in still water.

Hook	#12 XL/S
Tail	Dyed olive partridge
Body	Blended green laser-lights or similar ribbed with copper wire
Thorax	As for body with strands picked out for legs
Wing case	Olive pheasant tail
Eyes	Small black.

BROWN MUDEYE

This was a fly I tied commercially for many years and is a variant of one tied by Lindsay 'Hassa' Haslem, a renowned fly dresser and rod maker, who ran a tackle store in Richmond and later Hampton in Victoria, before moving to Tasmania to live.

Hook	#8
Body	Originally, Harris Tweed cloth that was unravelled, it was mostly dark brown but with fibres of green, navy and yellow. Later when I had used it all up and couldn't get more, I used brown or olive chenille.
Eyes	Black glass beads
Head	As for body
Note	After forming the body two beads are threaded onto the head material and after positioning are superglued into place. The remaining thread is tied 'figure eight' fashion to form the head before tying off

KINITOSHI MUDEYE

The 'Kinitoshi' or 'midnight mudeye' was given to me by Michael Griffiths. Mike was a tackle advisor in fly-fishing shops around Melbourne for many years.

Hook	#8
Tail	Small bunch of dyed olive kangaroo fur
Body	Dyed olive kangaroo fur
Eyes	Black mono eyes
Head	Dubbed olive kangaroo tied figure 8 style around the eyes

CORDULIID MUDEYE

This famous fly is the work of Fred Dunford, best known for his skill and knowledge of fishing Lake Eucumbene. This pattern is from his book *"Time of the Take"* published in 2012. He describes it as a flat-back sub-meniscus fly. It is widely used and successful.

Hook	#8
Body	Hare's ear dubbing
Wing	2 lots of 2 pairs of black duck breast feathers tied in separately
Legs	Deer hair
Head cover	Two small black duck breast feathers by the tips
Head	Trimmed ends of the deer hair head over-dubbed with poly-dubbing
Head cover	Pulled down pair of duck breast feathers and tied off

CROCHETED MUDEYE

Since Toril Kolbu came up with the idea of crocheted bodies it has been applied to numerous other flies. This one was provided by Neil Baillie.

Hook	#6-8 L/S.
Tail	Goose biots
Underbody	Lead wire tied along the shank to give extra width and cemented
Body	Crocheted Swannundaze
Legs	Goose biots
Wing case	Varnished quail pulled forward
Eyes	Glass beads
Head	Chenille

MC SHAG

An older Mudeye pattern I am told was created by the late Maury Wilson for Lake Wendouree in Ballarat. It was also known as Arch's Mudeye, but it seems to have failed the test of time and is not well known.

Hook	#8
Body	Black wool
Wing	Cormorant or black swan neck feathers tied flat over the body
Eyes	Black glass beads
Head	Thin black chenille

ROYCE'S MUDEYE.

From old and valued friend, and fellow Australian team member Dr Royce Baxter of Ballarat.

Hook	#6-8 Heavy wire
Tail	Black squirrel tied short
Body	Beige chenille
Wing	Brown partridge or quail flank
Head	Dark brown chenille

FLOATING MUDEYE

Origin unknown.

Hook	L/S 10
Back	3mm olive closed cell foam cut 9mm wide. Also forms the head
Body	Olive chenille
Legs	Barred green rubber
Head	3mm olive foam trimmed to shape

SHIRALEE

A very famous pattern first created in 1986 by Rick Keam. Rick made these commercially in the hundreds for tackle stores. He notes that the kangaroo hide must be chrome tanned as ordinary tanning leaves the leather too soft and it loses its shape. The relative buoyancy of 'roo' fur is also important to the fly's performance. The kangaroo hide is cut along the axis line of the fur (not across it) using a customised press knife and trimmed to shape both vertically and horizontally. Rabbit fur is totally unsuitable.

Hook	#6-10 L/S
Body	Unspecified but appears to be a double layer of tan cotton or similar with the kangaroo hide tied flat over top
Legs	Dyed brown, wood duck or Guinea fowl
Wingcase	Peacock herl
Eyes	Thick acrylic macramé yarn

THE BUG

A realistic 'bug' mudeye pattern I tied for the night hatches on Hepburn Lagoon. It worked well. Original? Probably not

Hook	#8-10
Body	Blended green seal fur
Waist	Two turns of brown partridge
Eyes	Burnt nylon. Or preformed plastic
Head	Olive blend dubbing

THE PATRIOT

A Mick Hall variant on a woolly bugger. He has used it in Eildon Pondage and caught and released a rainbow trout of 79cm and around 5.5kg taken on the actual sample fly he provided to me and shown here.

Hook	Kamasan B200 #6-8
Tail	A large bunch of olive rabbit fur
Body	Flat gold tinsel ribbed with gold wire
Wing	Olive Rabbit flared right around the body
Eyes	Gold bead chain
Head	Dubbed olive rabbit fur

BASS ROACH

Jeff Brown, a guide from Emu Plains in NSW gave me this pattern, thanks Geoff. I have tried it in lakes at night for trout and bass, and it works. The fly is either fished dead drift or on slow water using a slow retrieve with fairly long pauses. It may also be tied in smaller sizes for night time mudeye fishing.

Hook	#4-10
Tail	Black deer hair
Underbody	Black deer hair, palmered with clipped dark grizzle hackle
Wing	3 large black hen feathers tied flat
Head	Black deer hair trimmed slider style

BI-VISIBLE (BROWN)

Origins unknown.

Hook	#12-16
Tail	Brown cock hackle fibres
Body	Peacock herl is optional
Body	Two fully palmered brown cock hackle feathers back to back
Face	Two turns of white cock hackle

BI-VISIBLE (BLACK)

A favourite fly of English origin. Try it also in brown.

Hook	#12-14
Tail	Brown cock hackle fibres
Body	Four black cock hackles tied two at a time back to back and compressed
Hackle	Two turns of white cock

BIBIO

A fly of Irish origin widely used as a top dropper on 'Loch Style' rigs. Originally all black in colour, it has morphed into claret and black, and sometimes red and black. This fly is successful on lakes when mayfly duns are hatching. Because of its bulk, it creates a nice wake, and claret colour is widely used for duns and emergers as a top dropper fly. Its popularity is based on its success.

Hook	#10-14
Tail	None
Body	Black seal fur with the middle third claret
Rib	Silver wire
Hackle	Black cock slightly larger at the front

BLACK ANT 

Ants are regular fare for fish as they are part of the ecology for lurps living in Eucalypts that overhang streams. The ants' role is to spread the young lurps to new growth and in return they lick a sugary secretion as their reward. The ants frequently fall off into the water and are eagerly taken by trout. Ants can be red or brown but are more often black. There is no regular season for ants.

Hook	#12-16
Body	Black thread or fine dubbing
Wings	White hackle points, optional for flying ants
Hackle	Small black cock at the waist
Head	Black thread

BLACK CRICKET 

I first tied this fly for nighttime use in the 1960's during a cricket plague. It worked well too. It can be weighted with lead wire to fish during the day as trout seem to like it well sunk at this time. A variant of this fly supplied by Hilton Garcia has a clipped black deer hair head with some of long fibres left as legs. Hilton came from Sunbury, Victoria, where there are lots of crickets in the late summer. In the early days I used black plastic onion bag for legs, but this caused the fly to spin and twist the leader.

Hook	#6-8
Ovipositor	Black onion bag or round black plastic
Body	Dark brown chenille
Legs	Knotted black crow wing fibres
Head	Dark brown chenille

BLACK DOUGLAS 

This fly is from the late Athol Brown, a flyfisher and close friend of Trevor Hawkins. Athol owned a property on the Acheron River in Victoria.

Hook	#12-14
Tail	Golden Pheasant tippets
Butt	Yellow cock hackle clipped short
Body	Black cock hackle clipped short
Hackle	Cochybondhu tied thickly

BOGONG BEAUTY

This pattern was supplied by Mick Hall of Ballarat. It is a fair representation of the Bogong moth

Hook	#8-12
Tail	Barred Plymouth-rock (grizzle) hackle fibres
Body	Dubbed brushtail possum fur tied thickly
Rib	Four turns of gold Lurex
Hackle	Barred Plymouth rock, tied heavy

BRISTOL HOPPER

A fly supplied by England world team member Lester Booth There are many colour variations of this fly that successfully imitate a crane fly. In Australia, black or orange are useful colours, especially orange at altitudes of 1000 metres or more.

Hook	#10-12
Body	Brown goose biots
Hackle	Brown cock
Thorax	Bronze peacock herl
Legs	Knotted pheasant tail or black crow wing fibres

BROWN HAIR WING

A favourite of W. A. (Bill) McCulloch that he uses on the Mitta Mitta River around Eskdale in Victoria.

Hook	#14
Tail	Brown cock hackle fibres
Body	Dubbed brown seal fur
Wing	White calf tail
Hackle	Brown cock

CARROT FLY

This english fly came to me from former Tasmanian trout guide Neil Grose. It is fished as the top dropper in a team of flies when loch-style fishing. I believe the orange version is taken for one of the caddis species that frequently have an orange colour to them. The fly is highly recommended by John Horsey, former England captain, who also recommends the fly in claret or red.

Hook	#10-12
Tail	Pearl Lure-Flash strip
Body	Tapered orange seal fur
Rib	Copper or gold wire
Hackle	Orange

CLARET CARROT FLY 

Another version of the carrot fly from Neil Grose. It is the same 'recipe' as the 'orange' carrot fly but using claret coloured material. This fly is taken as an emerging dun.

Hook	#10-12
Tail	Pearl Lure-Flash strip
Body	Tapered Claret seal fur
Rib	Copper or gold wire
Hackle	Claret

CICADA 

I tied some of these for an excellent angler "The Shark" Max Vereshaka, for one of his many trips to New Zealand. It imitates the prolific small cicada found there. The example here is brown, but it can be tied in other colours. Mainland Australia also has slightly larger grass cicadas favoured by trout. A version of this fly with clear wings and a black body is effective for these. Max is the only angler I know to win all four sessions in a major fly fishing championship.

Hook	#8 dry fly
Tail	Medium brown hackle about ½ shank length
Abdomen	Clipped brown deer hair
Hackle	Medium brown to represent legs
Head	As for abdomen
Eyes	Black nylon

CICADA 

A fly from Norman Marsh, a famous New Zealand angler and author, it was published in his book "*Trout Stream Flies of New Zealand*".

Hook	#8-12
Tail	Natural deer hair
Body	Clipped deer hair.
Wings	Badger hackle tips
Collar	Bronze peacock herl
Hackle	Rhode Island Red
Head	Clipped deer hair

SOUTH ISLAND CICADA 

Contributed by Geoff Hall from the Goulburn Valley Fly Fishing Centre in Victoria.

Hook	#10
Body	Green micro chenille
Wing	Holographic gift wrap string
Head	Yellow and green deer hair trimmed to shape

CORBI MOTH

A fly of Tasmanian origins that was developed in the 1970's by Noel Jetson. It is a good imitation of the adult form of the cutworm (also known as army worm) (Corbi) grub and also the mainland Bogong Moth.

Sadly, Bogong moths seem to be in serious decline. Perhaps this is due to climate change or the wide use of pesticides.

Hook	#8 long shank (the original flies tied by Noel used gold plated hooks)
Body	Clipped deer hair
Wing	Mottled turkey wing
Hackle	Brown partridge
Head	Peacock herl

CRANEFLY HOPPER

Hopper is the common English name for an adult cranefly, also known as daddy long legs. This fly was supplied by former English fly-fishing captain Geoff Clarkson.

I have used this fly locally with success.

Hook	#12 XLS
Tail	Black cock hackle
Body	Dubbed seal fur, tied sparce
Legs	Knotted brown turkey
Hackle	Medium brown cock

CRANEFLY BLACK

Also known as Daddy Long-Legs. I like this English fly skated in windy conditions.

Hook	10-12 L/S
Body	Black seal fur
Rib	Flat silver tinsel
Legs	Knotted crow flight feather fibres, 2 each side
Wings	Grizzle hackle points tied flat are optional
Hackle	Black cock

CRANEFLY LEGLESS

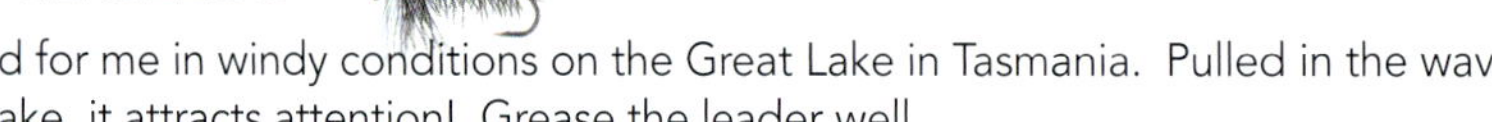

This fly has worked for me in windy conditions on the Great Lake in Tasmania. Pulled in the waves to leave a definite wake, it attracts attention! Grease the leader well.

Hook	#12 XL/S
Body	Black seal
Palmer	Short black hackle ribbed with silver wire
Hackle	Black cock
Face	Two turns of grizzle cock

CRANEFLY ORANGE

I won a couple of sessions on Rocky Valley Dam near Falls Creek in Victoria pulling this fly in a good breeze.

Hook	#12 L/S
Body	Dyed orange turkey quill ribbed with fine gold wire
Legs	Knotted orange turkey quill fibres. 2 each side
Hackle	Dyed hot orange grizzle

DUNNY BRUSH

A favourite fly of Jim Allen, of Compleat Angler store fame, it was created by Jim's good friend, Julian Brown. It was created by Julian to fish in the gathering darkness and night-time when Bogong Moths come out to fly. It is definitely not for daytime fishing. Bogong moths are juicy and very nutritious morsels and can be very prolific in the Australian High Country. They are eagerly taken by trout. This is a large fly and meant to be so. Fish it on lakes or slow pools in rivers, retrieve it to create a wake.

Hook	#4-8 wide gape
Tail	Natural black cock hackle
Body	Bronze peacock herl
Wings	Dark speckled turkey tied spent
Hackle	Plenty of large natural black cock

GOLD RIBBED HARE'S EAR

Hook	#12-16
Tail	Brown cock hackle
Body	Dubbed hare's ear fur ribbed with fine gold wire
Wing	Dark duck wing slips
Hackle	Brown

GREENWELL'S GLORY

A traditional English wet or dry fly that has claimed a great many fish for me and is one of my 'go to' flies for river fishing. The brainchild of a certain Cannon William Greenwell of Durham, it is the most famous fly of them all alongside the Royal Coachman.

Hook	#12-14
Tail	Nil
Body	Well waxed yellow thread. (when waxed the thread takes on an olive colour)
Rib	Fine gold wire
Wings	Duck wing slips
Hackle	Cochybondhu

HENRY'S BLEEDING STEELHEAD SKATER

From Alex S. Henry from Suskeena Lodge in British Columbia.

Hook	Low water #6-10
Tail	Pearl Crystal Flash
Body	Rear 2/3 claret seal fur, front 1/3 black
Rib	Embossed silver tinsel. (note - plain tinsel has been used for the fly shown)
Wing	Bleached elk hair or substitute

IRRESISTIBLE

A fly of American origin tied by Mr Joe Messenger. In his first version the body was halved. The lower half was white deer hair and the top half purple. The hackle was also purple. Later versions are more familiar like the Adam's Irresistible. The deer hair body makes for a very buoyant fly.

Hook	#8-16
Tail	Dark brown elk, deer or moose hair
Body	Spun and clipped natural deer hair
Wings	Grizzle hackle tips
Hackle	Mixed brown and grizzle

LATE NIGHT FINAL

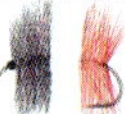

A once popular fly that seems to have faded into angling history. Promoted by Lance Wedlick as a 'go to' fly in fading light. The body is entirely made of compressed hackle. This is achieved by winding on a hackle feather and compacting from the front before adding another.

Hook	#8-12
Tail	White hackle
Body	Hackle tied in four sections. Rear section red, middle white, and front black, with a face hackle of three turns of white

PATE'S PANCORA

An Argentinian 'muddler' supplied by American Billy Pate who roams the world fly fishing. Pancora's are a freshwater crab, endemic to South America and Peru and eagerly taken by trout. These crabs might be part of the reason why there are such big fish over there?

Hook	#6 L/S
Body	Dubbed rabbit with guard hairs, tied plump
Wing	Peacock herl trimmed at twice the shank length.
Overwing	A wide brown cock hackle feather from the side of the neck
Head	Spun natural grey deer hair
Note	From the top view, the fly head looks round in shape, but it is actually trimmed very flat on the top and bottom

RAT FACE MCDOUGAL

One of those 'representing anything' flies that float and fish very well. Invented in USA by Harry Darby, it has spawned quite a few variants.

Hook #10-14
Tail Ginger cock hackle fibres or reddish deer hair
Body Clipped spun deer hair
Wings Grizzle hackle points
Hackle Ginger and grizzle mixed

ROD'S GREY STONE FLY

Supplied by Victorian guide Rod Barford. After completion, trim the hackle underneath so the fly will sit flat on the water.

Hook #14L/S
Body Grey Antron body palmered with small dark 'dun' hackle and trimmed on top so the wing will lie flat
Wing Single grey goose biot tied in point first and cut to length
Hackle Small dark dun

ROYAL COACHMAN

A personal favourite. It is widely attributed to Tom Bosworth, royal coach driver to George IV, and Queen Victoria, and a world-wide favourite fly. This was the first dry fly pattern that I tied that I caught a trout on, and there have been a great many fish since, hence my liking for it. Variants may have a different colour waist like orange, yellow or grey.

Hook #8-18
Tail Golden Pheasant tippets
Butt Peacock herl
Waist Red floss
Thorax Peacock herl
Wings A pair of matched white duck quill slips
Hackle Coachman brown

ROYAL WULFF

Invented by American Lee Wulff. This pattern was provided by Jack Dennis. I regard it as a variant on the Royal Coachman.

Hook #10-16
Tail Dark elk hair
Butt Peacock herl
Waist Red floss
Thorax Peacock herl
Wings White calf tail, upright and divided
Hackle Brown cock

SOFA PILLOW

One of those general high floating pattern flies that could represent a caddis, grasshopper or stonefly. I particularly like it in smaller sizes even though the Americans dress it on anything up to a #4. A change of body colour is all that's needed to alter its character.

Hook	#8-14
Tail	Deer hair
Body	Red, yellow or green seal fur or floss
Palmer	Dark grizzle cock
Wing	Deer hair
Hackle	Brown, red or grizzle cock tied full

SPLUTTER BUG FROG

Another bass fly from 'Cocky Bondhu'.

Hook	#4-6 X Wide gape
Weed guard	0kg mono (optional)
Legs	Each leg has 3 knotted strands from a rubber skirt
Body	Compacted stacks of deer hair with yellow underneath and other colours on top
Eyes	4-6mm stick-ons

SPRUCE FLY

This fly was given and recommended to me by my friend, the late Ray Clark, captain of the 1991 Australian fly fishing team. He included it in his personal 6 best ever flies published in 1997 in '*Australia's Best Trout Flies*'. I have fished this fly on small streams with great success.

Hook	#12-18
Tail	Moose body hair fibres
Body	Red floss
Thorax	Peacock herl
Wings	Badger hackle points
Hackle	Badger

TERMITE

During spring, in humid thundery weather termites at times hatch in the millions. Technically called 'Alates' they flutter away from the termite mounds to spread the species far and wide. Not being very good fliers, they frequently land on water, especially bush streams. Trout find these insects delectable and during a hatch, trout will stay up in the water column feeding on the surface to gobble them up in great numbers. Be careful not to 'line' a fish when casting to it. Colours can vary from cream through yellow to shades of brown.

Hook	#12
Body	Creamy yellow to light brown floss
Wings	Grizzle hackle points or clear packing string tied flat
Hackle	Pale grizzle trimmed off at the bottom

TERMITE PARACHUTE

The parachute version sits nice and flat on the water.

Hook	#12
Thread	Colour to suit
Body	Creamy yellow to light brown floss
Wing	Deer hair post tied short
Hackle	Pale grizzle tied parachute

TUTTLE MOUSE

Another Lance Wedlick fly. Mice are great swimmers and often migrate.

Crossing a river or stream is no problem for them, they just jump in and head across leaving a wake on the surface as they go. Fish this fly in a similar way and at a fair pace. Fish can swim far faster than any retrieve an angler can do. Fish see these rodents as a large nutritious meal to be jumped upon and eaten. Note: These flies use up a lot of deer hair. When tying, any underfur present it should be combed out

Hook	#6-8 XL/S
Tail	A slim bunch of marabou or a thin strip of leather
Body	Compacted deer hair. (trimmed to shape)
Ears	Leather cut outs
Eyes	Preformed nylon or beads on nylon

WOLLONDIBBY WONDER

Len Pawsey, an uncle of Mick Hall, is credited with this fly. It is also tied on standard wet fly hooks in sizes #10 – 12.

Hook	#8 low water salmon
Tail	A large bunch of red golden pheasant flank feathers
Body	Dubbed dark chocolate seal fur
Rib	Gold Lurex
Wings	Cock pheasant green rump tied killer style
Head	Deer hair trimmed to muddler shape

GRASSHOPPERS

ALBERTA HOPPER 

Bill Robertson, a Canadian world fly fishing team representative gave this pattern for use in his home state. The pattern seems interesting enough to try anywhere.

Hook	#8-10
Tail	Red deer hair tied short
Body	Wrapped yellow closed cell foam
Palmer	Brown cock hackle
Wing	Six strands of Crystal Flash under a bunch of deer hair
Head	Orange seals fur palmered with grizzle hackle

AUSTRALIAN GRASSHOPPER 

Another standard fly as described by F.A.D.G. Griffiths.

Hook	#6-10
Body	Lemon floss
Wing	Oak turkey, tied flat.
Legs	6 Golden Pheasant tippets either side of the wing and protruding 6mm beyond the hook bend.
Hackle	Natural grey cock

AUTUMN HOPPER 

One of Rick Keam's specialties. The body can be cut from pale cream foam or white foam that is coloured using a felt tip pen. Rick made the bodies in numbers and lightly singed them with a flame to get the right colouring. Fumes from this process can be problematic, so do it outside.

Hook	#12
Abdomen	Tapered closed cell foam
Legs	Tapered and knotted tan raffia
Head	Deer hair tied bullet head style and trimmed to leave a few strands ends as legs

BANJO'S HOPPER 

Designed by Peter Leuver, who has paid particular attention to the natural insects profile. Not a pretty fly, but drowned hoppers never are.

Hook	#10-12
Tail	Red wool as for a red tag
Body	Brown/grey deer hair tapered so that the tail becomes part of the body
Wing	Golden Pheasant tippets tied in a vertical fan shape
Legs	Knotted Golden Pheasant centre tail fibres
Head	Deer hair

BREDBO

Believed to be the first original Australian tied fly pattern, circa 1896, and regularly quoted as such. It was named after the Bredbo River in southern NSW. Tied in the traditional English wet fly style it has a long history as a fish catcher.

Hook	#12
Body	Yellow floss
Rib	Medium gold wire
Sides	Golden Pheasant tippets
Wing	Mottled turkey or hen pheasant wing
Hackle	Brown partridge

BULLET HEAD HOPPER

One of a large number of flies with this style head. They float well and fish even better.

Hook	#10-12
Body	Pale green seal fur dubbing
Legs	Golden Pheasant tippets
Wing	Two slips of mottled turkey or hen pheasant wing
Head	Deer or elk hair tied forward then pulled back
Legs	Fibres left from trimmed head

BERCHDOLT'S HOPPER

Mr. George Berchdolt originator. The fly shown is an original 'Berchdolt Hopper' as supplied by John Brookes.

Hook	#8-12
Tail	Golden Pheasant tippets
Body	Pale olive wool
Rib	Blanket stitched yellow floss
Wing	Cock pheasant green rump feathers
Hackle	Orange cock
Face hackle	Cock Pheasant green rump feather

BUTTERWORTH'S HOPPER

The late Ray Butterworth, a guide from Flowerdale in Victoria, who fished the legendary King Parrot Creek, invented this fly. The foam body ensures its floating capabilities.

Hook	#12
Back	A strip of light brown Etha foam
Body	Yellow/green floss
Hackle	Light brown cock
Head	Continuation of the back and trimmed

CROCHETED HOPPER

Tied by Stephen Chatterton in 1998 to keep up with the then current theme of crocheted bodied flies.

Hook	#8
Body	Crocheted wool
Wing	Crystal flash under grey deer hair
Head	Deer hair

DETACHED BODY HOPPER

A favourite pattern of Australian angling artist Trevor Hawkins.

Hook	Size 14 or 12 up-eye dry fly
Body	Plastic mayfly body
Legs	Golden Pheasant tippets
Head	Deer or elk hair tied muddler or bullet head style

DOCTOR WARK

A famous Victorian fly invented by long deceased Melbourne dentist of the same name.

Hook	#10-12
Tail	Guinea feather fibres (Galena)
Body	Green Lurex
Rib	Gold wire
Wings	White hackle tips at right angles to shank
Hackle	Pale ginger

GIBBO HOPPER

Named after the Gibbo River near Benambra in Victoria. This fly was designed by Ray Clarke, a former Australian fly fishing team captain from Paynesville, who often fished in the area up around Omeo.

Hook	#8-10
Body	Yellow or green deer hair wrapped with latex
Legs	Golden Pheasant tippets
Head	Deer hair

GLEN INNES HOPPER 

Origin unknown. From the Glen Innes district of northern NSW perhaps?

Hook	#12
Body	Yellow chenille
Wings	Two badger hackle points, and a strip of dyed red duck quill
Hackle	Grizzle

GOVERNOR'S INDESTRUCTIBLE 

Modelled on Ernest Schweibert's 'Letort' hopper, this reliable and durable fly was developed by Lieut. Gen. Sir Donald Dunstan, (former commander of the Australian Army), to have the correct profile and float well.

Hook	#10-12
Body	Blended yellow, brown and red seal fur
Wing	Oak turkey with a coat of Flexi cement
Legs	Red deer hair with some yellow
Head	Clipped deer hair

GRIFFITHS GRASSHOPPER 

This is 'Fadg' Griffiths version of the grasshopper tied in an unusual way.

Hook	Small low water salmon hook
Tail	A tuft of orange floss
Body	Tied rather thick, rear ½ yellow floss, with a
Golden	Pheasant tippet in the middle of the body, with four fibres either side of the body. The front half of the body is then made from yellow floss
Hackle	Red and grizzle cock wound together

HACKLE HOPPER 

A proven Australian hopper pattern that was commercially tied a minimum of 50 years ago by J.M Gillies but of unknown origin. The original Gillies pattern is:

Hook	#10-12
Tail	Golden pheasant tippets
Body	Rear half silver tinsel, front half brown chenille
Palmer	Red cock hackle
Hackle	A small Golden Pheasant feather wound as hackle

HACKLE HOPPER

A more modern version of the above.

Hook	#12
Tail	GP tippets
Body	Flat gold tinsel
Palmer	Pale ginger hackle
Face hackle	A small Golden Pheasant feather wound as hackle

HENRYS FORK HOPPER

This contribution is from well known American angler and fly tyer Mike Lawson, whom I met in Melbourne some years ago.

Hook	#10 L/S
Body	Clipped light elk or deer hair
Wing	Yellow deer hair
Head	Deer hair trimmed to shape

LADE'S HOPPER 

Bill Lade from Adelaide supplied this hopper pattern he uses on the Thredbo River in NSW.

Hook	#10
Body	Dubbed seal fur, 50% orange and 50% green
Legs	Golden pheasant tippets
Head	Clipped grey deer hair

NOEL'S KNOBBY HOPPER 

Noel's Knobby. A now universally known fly by the late Noel Jetson of Tasmania.

Hook	#12 L/S
Body	Yellow chenille
Wing	Bunch of golden pheasant tippets
Head	Deer fur trimmed muddler style

O'BRIEN'S HOPPER

Other than the name, the origins of this fly remain a mystery. The use of a woodcock feather doesn't help either. Woodcocks are a largish sandpiper common in Eurasia and the America's but there is no Australian species. The body feather is red-brown, and it is substituted with male wood duck flank.

Hook	#8-12
Body	Yellow chenille
Wing	A single small Golden Pheasant tippet feather tied flat
Hackle	A woodcock's feather or wood duck flank

ROB'S BEAD HEAD HOPPER

One I claim for myself. I fish it like a bead head nymph with great success in fast riffles during 'hopper' time. There are 2 versions, one with a chenille body and the other with light green Sparkle Dubbing.

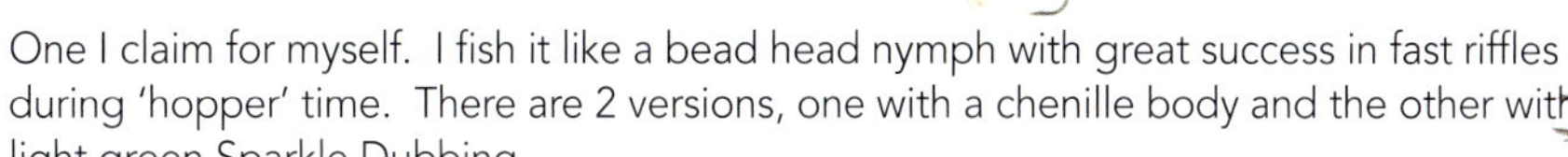

Hook	#10
Underbody	Lead wire
Tail	Golden Pheasant tippet
Body	Yellow chenille or light green Sparkle Dubbing
Wing	Golden Pheasant tippets tied behind the head
Bead	Brass
Hackle	Orange hen tied in front of the bead

SMARTS HOPPER

I have no idea who Smart is, but here is the hopper pattern.

Hook	#12
Tail	Dyed red duck wing slip
Body	Natural raffia
Wing	Hen pheasant
Hackle	Grizzle with brown partridge at the front

THREDBO HOPPER

As used by Mr. Bill Lade, an Adelaide angler.

Hook	#10
Tail	Nil
Body	Dubbed green seal fur
Wing	Golden Pheasant Tippet and grey deer hair
Head	Spun deer hair, muddler style

WET GRASSHOPPER

Another popular wet hopper that I have found useful.

Hook	#10
Underbody	Lead wire
Body	Pale olive wool
Legs	Knotted red goose quill
Wing	Golden Pheasant tippets
Wing	Grey duck quill strips
Hackle	Natural red hen

WHOPPER

An American hopper with a very realistic profile and colours to match Australian hoppers.

Hook	#8-10
Body	Closed cell foam in pale green or brown
Underwing	Yellow Deer or elk hair
Overwing	Lacquered cock pheasant 'church window' feather tied flat
Legs	Knotted clumps of red Golden Pheasant fibres
Head	Deer hair tied bullet style

WILSON'S SIMPLE HOPPER

Designed by that great Victorian authority on Australian flies, the late Maury Wilson. It is a simple but effective fly that Maury suggested should be splashed down on the water to imitate the splash landing of a grasshopper. This is generally good advice when 'hopper' fishing.

Hook	8-12
Body	Yellow/green tying thread
Wing	A clump of Golden Pheasant tippets tied flat
Hackle	Mixed brown and grizzle cock

MATUKAS

Not to be confused with the Matuku also listed here. How the change of name came about is not known. Like some other flies it can be tied in almost any colour. Yellow is good for dirty water and white works well in bright conditions. Darker colours suit failing or low light. It's unlikely there is a combination of colours that hasn't been tried. The golden rule being: 'The darker the light the darker the fly, the brighter the light the paler the fly'. One of the problems with Matuka fishing is short takes from the trout. A lot of fly Tyers make the tails too long. Tails on these flies should be the same length as the hook shank or even a bit shorter. I remember well some 55 years ago tying a batch of what I thought were perfect red and black matukas for one of the best anglers I ever saw, the late Alan Walker of Hobart. He looked at them, thanked me, commented how nicely they were tied, then promptly got a pair of scissors and cut the tails off just beyond the round of the hook. *Lesson Learned!* I sometimes also use a head hackle, a lead wire underbody, a metal beadhead, or both. Jungle cock eye feathers and or a single strand of crystal flash along the centre of the tail are excellent additions also.

BLACK AND RED MATUKA

Hook	#2-10
Body	Red wool
Rib	Silver oval or flat tinsel
Wing	2 or 4 feathers from a black hen cape tied back to back
Head	Black varnish

EARLY SEASON MATUKA

A Lance Wedlick recommendation for use in dirty water. Yellow is often seen in barramundi flies for use in dirty water, and it works just as well on trout.

Hook	#6-8
Body	White floss or seal fur
Rib	Narrow silver flat tinsel
Wing	Two yellow hen saddle feathers back to back
Hackle	Red hen

GREEN MATUKA

This is one of the few matuka's I tie with cock hackle wings rather than hen. The reason for the black tail is that many of our smelt show black at the vent.

Hook	#6-10
Tail	Black cock hackle fibres
Body	Blended green seal with highlights
Rib	Gold wire
Wing	Four dyed green Cree cock hackles
Hackle	Green Cree cock (optional)

INCREDIBLE SILVER MINNOW

Hook	6-8 L/S
Underbody	Fine lead wire
Body	White floss ribbed with silver tinsel
Wing	White Bucktail with 3 strands of blue on either side
Overwing	Grey mallard breast tied flat as in a Craig's night-time pattern
Head	Built up thread and well varnished
Eyes	Black and yellow Stick-Ons

JACK'S SPRATT

Mr. Jack English, a tackle store owner from the Tongariro River in New Zealand came up with this good smelt imitation. Like all fishing to smelting fish, it is hard work and can be very frustrating. Now you see them, now you don't, and they often turn up a little later 10 metres or more away. These 'smelting' fish are usually travelling fast. Try and guess which way they are going and present the fly as quickly as you can. Cast well out front and hope you've got it right.

Hook #4-8
Body Flat silver tinsel
Rib Fine silver flat wire
Wing Badger hackles back to back and tied down matuka style

MATUKA MINNOW

Hook #6-8
Underbody Fine lead wire
Body Red seal fur
Wing Two furnace cock hackle overlaid with another two Cree hackles on either side
Side fins Cree hackle points
Eyes Bead chain

PARSONS GLORY

Another Kiwi fly that works here in Australia. Invented by a Philip Parsons, it is also a good smelt pattern and looks a lot like a baby trout.

Hook #4-8
Body Yellow chenille
Rib Silver tinsel
Wing Well marked honey grizzle hackle, tied back to back matuka style
Throat Orange hackle whisks
Eyes Jungle cock eyes are optional

HORROR

Buschy's Horror. A Kaj Busch invention. What a fly, talk about an unusual innovation. Based on a traditional matuka tie, the palmered hackle imparts extra life and movement. A number of colour variations are productive.

Hook #6-8
Body Black chenille
Wing Four brown cock hackles
Rib Oval silver tinsel
Palmer Brown or black cock tied in at the tail end and wound forward

MINI REDFIN

Hook #12-14
Tail Red hackle points
Body Green Seal fur blend
Rib Copper wire
Wing Four dyed green Cree hen back to back
Hackle Two turns of red hen hackle

RED ARSED BASTARD LONGTAIL

This fly bears a strong resemblance to Wigram's Robin fly except for the rather heavy hackle.

Hook #6-10 mostly 8
Tail Red floss
Butt Red floss
Thorax Peacock herl
Rib Fine gold wire
Wing 2 pairs cock hackle tips back to back and matched at the ends
Note The wing is wound down matuka style only at the thorax area
Hackle Rather log black cock

RED THROATED WHITEBAIT

Hook #6-10 XL/S
Body Grey wool
Wing Cree cock hackle feathers
Rib Flat silver tinsel
Throat Red hackle fibres

ROBIN

The invention of Tasmanian fly fishing legend Dick Wigram. This is a personal favourite of mine. I was given an original fly tied by Mr Wigram himself, and he used the spade feathers from the side of a cock hackle cape.

Hook #8-10
Body Halved, rear half fluorescent red wool, front half black seal.
Rib Gold wire to front half only.
Wing Black spade cock or hen cape feathers. (Tied in so that the tail section of the fly 'kicks' up slightly to avoid the tail wrapping around the hook as is common in many longtail flies)
Eyes Jungle cock eyes

SONIC MATUKA

From South Australian angler Dave Bennett, who designed this fly to create water disturbance or movement. I have tied it in red and black, plain black, and also green with good results. A weighted version is good in lakes.

Hook	#6
Body	Gold Lurex wrap
Rib	Gold wire
Wings	2 pairs Grizzle hen hackle feathers dyed green
	Note the wings are splayed outwards
Gills	Red marabou

MATUKU

An old New Zealand fly originally made from Bittern feathers. The name deriving from the Maori name for the bird. Bitterns or Night Herons are now totally protected, and as such, the feathers can be substituted with hen pheasant feathers.

Hook	#6-10
Body	Red or yellow wool
Wing	Two hen pheasant flank feathers tied back to back
Rib	Fine silver oval tinsel

Australia has over 200 known species of mayfly from nine different families.

"*Atalophlebia Australis*" A. Australis is the most common "March Brown" mayfly and widespread on both the southern Australian mainland and Tasmania. They are represented here in many of the fly patterns. The other species found in Tasmania are: A superba. A. *albiterminata* and species of *Atalonella* and *Tasmanophlebia*. There are many other lesser known species also.

ADAMS

An American fly invented by Les Halliday in the 1920's and named after a friend. It was originally tied with spent wings. It can also be tied as a parachute hackle and this version is one of my 'go to' flies when small duns are on the water. A small olive version can be very effective when olive duns are hatching.

Hook	#12-18 commonly #14-16
Thread	Grey
Wings	Grizzle hackle points
Post	Grey or white Hi-Viz or similar. (If being tied parachute fashion)
Tail	Mixed brown & grizzle hackle fibres
Body	Dubbed muskrat
Hackle	Mixed brown & grizzle

ASH DUN

Thanks to Ashley Artis from Devonport, Tasmania for this fly of his.

Hook	#12
Tail	Chocolate dun hackle fibres
Body	Stripped natural peacock herl
Thorax	Grey/brown superfine dubbing
Wings	Matched pair of grey duck wing slips
Hackle	Dark dun

ASH DUN NO HACKLE

Another Ashley Artis creation. Ashley's idea of splitting the tail is excellent. For some reason duns tied with split tails fish much better. This technique should be applied to all dry dun patterns.

Hook	#10-12
Tail	Chocolate dun hackle fibres split
Body	Stripped peacock herl
Wings	Two matching duck quill slips
Thorax	Fine brown dubbing

BIOT PARACHUTE

An entry 20 years ago from M. Howard, a person I cannot recall. (Apologies).

Hook	#12-16
Body	Green goose biot
Post	Hi-Viz
Thorax	Olive dubbing
Hackle	Olive cock

BLUE DUN

A Standard English pattern that has proved its worth many times.

Hook	#12-14
Tail	Blue dun hackle fibres
Body	Dubbed mole fur
Wings	Duck quill slips
Hackle	Blue dun cock

CAENIS

John Rumpf. Everybody knows of "Rumpfy's" legendary fishing and casting skills, and many of his flies. John is an Australian fly fishing representative with a huge repertoire of techniques and knowledge that he readily shares.

Hook	#20-28
Tail	3 Iron blue hackle fibres
Body	Dubbed white rabbit
Wings	White Hi-Viz, tied flat
Thorax	Fine black dubbing

CAENID

Origin unknown. The person who gave this fly did not write his name, but suggested the leader be well greased to within 20cm of the fly. Another version of this fly uses white raffia cut in a circular shape and split.

Hook	# 14-20
Tail	Black cock
Body	Very sparse black superfine dubbing
Wing	Teased out pearl tinsel thread
Hackle	2 turns only very small grizzle

CLARET DUN

A favourite fly of Barrie Smith from Melbourne, a guest at the 1996 world fly fishing championships. It was mostly used at London Lakes, Tasmania, where he had a house, and around the Tasmanian Highlands.

Hook	#12
Tail	Claret hackle fibres
Body	Dubbed claret seals fur ribbed with short claret hackle
Wings	Brown turkey wing slips
Hackle	Claret and grizzle mixed

DEER DUN

I especially like the look of this Jan Spencer fly, and have tied some but not used them yet. I have varied the material on some to make the body from cock pheasant centre tail that matches the March Browns.

Hook	#12
Tail	Natural deer hair
Body	Brown thread
Rib	Fine copper wire
Wing	Natural deer hair
Legs	Natural deer hair extended from the wings
Head	Peacock herl

FUNNEL DUN

Ezra Bibby. A fly that seems to work well on the Kiewa River in Victoria. Also tie it in smaller sizes in olive when those mayflies are about.

Hook	#12-14
Tail	Hackle fibres twice as long as the hook
Body	Fine dubbing
Hackle	Oversize and swept forward by the thorax
Thorax	Darker dubbing than the body

BROWN BIOT

Another favourite from Ashley Artis.

Hook	#12-14
Tail	Cockybondhu
Body	Brown goose biot
Thorax	Brown superfine dubbing
Hackle	Cochybondhu

HAYSTACK

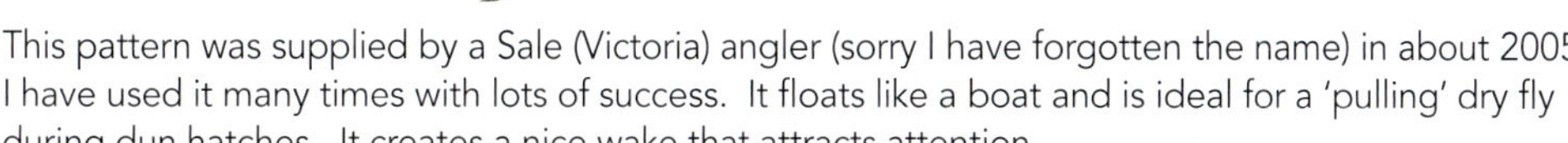

This pattern was supplied by a Sale (Victoria) angler (sorry I have forgotten the name) in about 2005. I have used it many times with lots of success. It floats like a boat and is ideal for a 'pulling' dry fly during dun hatches. It creates a nice wake that attracts attention.

Hook	#12-14
Tail	Deer hair
Body	Dubbed hare's ear or rabbit fur with guard hairs
Wing	Spun deer hair flared out in a half circle

HIGHLAND DUN

This fly is by the late Noel Jetson formerly of Cressy, Tasmania.

Hook	#10 down eye
Tail	Small bunch of Rhode Island Red hackle feathers
Body	Brown floss silk palmered with a small Rhode Island Red hackle
Rib	Bronze wire
Wings	Matched pair of brown speckled hen wing strips
Hackle	Mixed grizzle and Rhode Island Red

IRON BLUE DUN 

So many of our proven patterns are of English origin and this is yet another. In small sizes it is a Baetis representation, or in larger sizes one of the darker duns. Either way it catches fish.

Hook	#12-16
Tail	Blue dun cock hackle fibres
Butt	Red floss
Body	Dubbed Mole fur
Wing	Duck wing slips
Hackle	Iron blue dun

JASON'S DUN

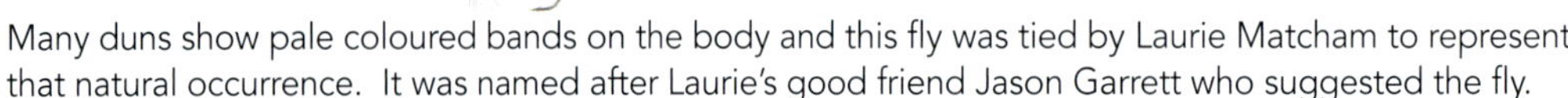

Many duns show pale coloured bands on the body and this fly was tied by Laurie Matcham to represent that natural occurrence. It was named after Laurie's good friend Jason Garrett who suggested the fly.

Hook	#12-14
Tail	Brown hackle fibres
Body	Cock pheasant centre tail fibres
Rib	White floss strand
Wing	Brown hen pheasant slips or brown speckled hen
Hackle	A light brown and blue dun wound together

JAYS DUN CADDIS 

A fly supplied by Jay Buckner, a regular skipper of a number of the USA world fly fishing teams. A fly that he said fishes well on evening rises to spent caddis. Note: There are many Australian small dark caddis that would be well imitated by a #16-18 version of this fly.

Hook	#12
Body	A few strands of dark grey goose quill
Wings	Two strips darkest duck quill tied tent like over body and coated with flex cement
Antennae	Two fine stripped hackle points
Hackle	Chocolate dun and grizzle mixed

KAKAHI QUEEN 

Favoured by "The Shark" Max Vereshaka, who likes it as a general mayfly pattern.
It also comes in a wet version.

Hook	#10-14
Tail	Furnace hackle fibres
Body	Stripped peacock herl
Wing	Mallard slips with a few teal breast feather stands dyed or marked yellow
Hackle	Furnace

KOZZY DUN

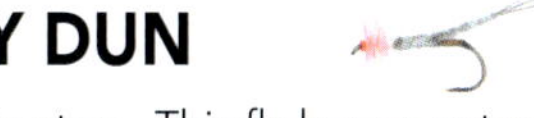

Andrew Overton. This fly has an extended body, the first part (made separately) being tied on the tail before placement on the hook. Andrew ties this fly with 'paraloop' hackles on either side of the hook. This is a difficult process, conventional hackle is much easier and produces a similar result.

Hook	#12
Tail	Ginger elk mane
Body	Dubbed muskrat
Wings	Grey feather from a French partridge
Thorax	As for body
Hackle	Ginger

LYNE'S FANCY

This fly is of Tasmanian origin and created by the late and famous Reg Lyne. This is a favourite pattern of an old friend Jason Garrett, who served as captain of Australian teams at world fly fishing championships and was my captain in Czesky Krumlov in 1996 (fond memories). This fly was the first highland dun he ever fished. He used it first in 1948 at Little Pine Lagoon, Tasmania, and it is still a favourite of his even though it is not so well known these days.

Hook	#12 up eye.
Tail	Furnace brown
Body	Stripped peacock herl
Wing	Jason uses dark turkey, but the original fly used furnace hackle points.
Hackle	Furnace cock hackle

MCLAUGHLIN MARVEL

Source unknown, but this is a more than useful fly on the NSW Monaro River of the same name.

Hook	#12-14
Tail	Black hackle fibres
Body	Dubbed red fox fur
Hackle	Cree

OMNI

Invented by Michael Ball. There are 6 versions of this fly in "Australia's Best Trout Flies'. I have chosen the one I like best, 'Big Mac' but it works in smaller sizes.

Hook	10 -14
Thread	Brown
Butt	A small bunch of brown Antron
Tail	Two bunches of red cock hackle fibres split either side of the butt
Body	Brown thread
Rib	Fine red copper wire
Rear hackle	Small red cock
Hackle	Red and grizzle compacted as it is tied in

PARA DUN

One of four flies given by Andrew Overton.

Hook	#16
Tail	Brown hackle fibres
Body	Dubbed hares ear fur
Rib	Fine copper wire
Post	Yellow floss.
Thorax	As for body
Hackle	Brown & grizzle wound on post.
Note	After the hackle is tied down the post is pulled down firmly and tied off at the eye of the hook

PECK'S DUN

Charles Peck from Launceston, Tasmania is the originator of this fly. An effective imitation for March Browns.

Hook	#10-12
Tail	Dark chocolate hackle fibres
Body	Brown thread
Ribbing	Brown thread
Palmer	Small brown hackle
Wing	Oak Turkey
Hackle	Chocolate brown and grizzle

POSSUM FUR FLY

Made entirely of possum fur, it was given to me by Keith Credland of Wynyard Tasmania. His use of the oily fur at the base of the possum's tail makes the fly very buoyant.

Hook	#12-14 Tiemco
Tail	Black possum tail fibres
Body	Dubbed light grey fur from the base of a possum's tail
Thorax	Dubbed dark fur from a possum tail
Wing	Base hair from a possum tail. It is tied in by the tips with the light grey ends upward. The wing is tied in front of the thorax.

RUSTY PARA DUN

Supplied by David Pickering of the Goulburn Valley Fly Fishing Centre. He fishes it during dun hatches and spinner falls, using it in bubble lines and on flat water.

Hook	12-16
Tail	3 or 4 long hackle fibres
Body	Rusty brown Antron
Rib	Fine gold wire
Post	Honey coloured Hi-Viz
Hackle	Ginger

SEPIA DUN

David Cameron from Hamilton in Victoria gave me this fly that he uses on Lake Hamilton for the *"A. Australis"* dun hatches there.

Hook	#12
Tail	Black hackle fibres
Body	Dubbed blended black and red seal fur
Rib	Copper wire
Hackle	Black cock tied forward for the dun or backward for the emerger

TWILIGHT BEAUTY

Originated in New Zealand by Basil Humphrey.

Hook	#10-14
Tail	Ginger cock
Body	Black floss
Wing	Duck quill slips
Hackle	Ginger cock

YARRA DUN

Generally, only seen singly, these are the biggest duns I have ever seen. Usually fluttering near the surface, likely laying eggs. I suspect they may be 'Mirawara' duns. The nymphs of these are the biggest yet discovered in Australia, the nymphs being up to 25mm long. The hackles are all trimmed underneath so the fly rides low on the water.

Hook	#10 -12
Tail	Three black micro fibbets or elk hair fibres well spread
Body	Dubbed ginger rabbit
Rib	Fine gold wire
Palmer	Palest short ginger cock
Wing	Sparse pale deer hair
Hackle	Pale ginger cock

MAYFLY EMERGERS

BARRY LODGE EMERGER

Designed by Barry Lodge to float in the meniscus with deadly effect during dun hatches. It has become a favourite fly in Tasmania and the Western Lakes of Victoria.

Hook	#10-14
Tail	Red cock hackle fibres
Body	Chocolate dubbing
Rib	Copper wire
Wing	Starling or duck tied spent or at 45 degrees
Thorax	Chocolate dubbing
Hackle	Dark brown cock, two turns only

BRAESIDE EMERGER

From guide John Pincombe from Merrijig, Victoria. This fly is fished to emerger feeders in fast water, as a single fly or behind an indicator.

Hook	#14
Tail	3 strands cock pheasant centre tail
Body	Thin copper wire
Wing case	Dark strip of black duck flight feather
Thorax	Dubbed rabbit including guard hairs
Hackle	3 turns grizzle saddle

BROWN NYMPH EMERGER

Rod Barford's take on this regular pattern.

Hook	#12-14
Tail	Red cock hackle
Body	Dubbed brown seal fur
Rib	Fine gold wire
Wing	Brown partridge wonder wing
Thorax	As for body

CLARET EMERGER

A favoured fly of Englishman Jeremy Herman, a former world champion fly fisher. He uses it on still water.

Hook	Kamasan B170 #12
Thread	Black
Body	Dark claret seal fur
Rib	Fine pearl Lurex
Hackle	Red game and clipped underneath

GREY POSSUM TAIL

From well-known Tasmanian fly fisher Tony Dell. This fly was supplied as his sample.

Hook	#12-16
Body	Dubbed possum underfur ribbed with flat gold tinsel
Wing	Black fibres from the base of a possum tail Stacked in a hair stacker
Hackle	Originally black and white cock hackles wound together or alternatively short dark grizzle

DOWN-UNDER EMERGER

From Michael Winterton, formerly of the Alpine Angler store.

Hook	#10-12 Caddis bend
Tail	Possum tail
Body	Dubbed dark possum fur
Wing	Brown partridge
Thorax	As for body
Hackle	Brown cock trimmed short

FOAM EMERGER

Provided by Tasmanian John O'Halloran. He uses it on Tasmanian Highland Lakes for Highland dun hatches.

Hook	#12
Tail	Fiery brown hackle fibres
Body	Dubbed brown seal fur
Wing	Grey closed cell foam trimmed to shape
Thorax	As for body
Hackle	Fiery brown tied parachute

KLINKHAMMER SPECIAL

Now world famous, this fly is the work of Dutchman, Hans Van Klinken. Most fly boxes would have a version of this fly in at least one of its many variants.

Hook	#10-12 Mustad GRS12ST or K12ST or similar
Body	Light or dark tan or rusty olive
Wing post	White Poly Yarn (I use Hi-Viz)
Thorax	Three strands peacock herl
Hackle	Hans prefers blue dun, but also uses brown or light ginger

MALLARD AND CLARET

A traditional English wet fly that catches well in waters where duns occur. In suitable weather when a dun hatch is expected later in the day, this is a good choice during a pre-hatch, when nymphs become very active. Mallard is not an easy feather to use initially but perseverance will improve results. The feather fibres are rolled into a 6mm wide strip before tying in.

Hook	#12
Tail	Golden Pheasant tippets
Body	Claret wool
Rib	Fine gold oval tinsel
Wing	Bronze mallard shoulder feather
Hackle	Claret

MARCH BROWN PALMER

This is also a top dropper fly tied and supplied by master fly tier David Dodd from Ballarat. David's flies are very exact and of the highest standard.

Hook	TMC #12-14
Tail	Yellow wool tag
Body	Dubbed 75% hares ear fur and 25% orange seal fur
Rib	Fine gold wire
Palmer	Furnace hackle with 2 turns of brown partridge at the front

NEWLYN EMERGER

An emerging nymph pattern tied to imitate March Brown mayflies A Australis. It was provided by Peter Julian and used for the dun hatches on that lake near Ballarat. Be careful not to stretch the foam too tight over the thorax as it will cause the fly to sink. A small downward bend is added to hook shank about 5mm from the eye so the fly will float at the thorax and sink at the tail.

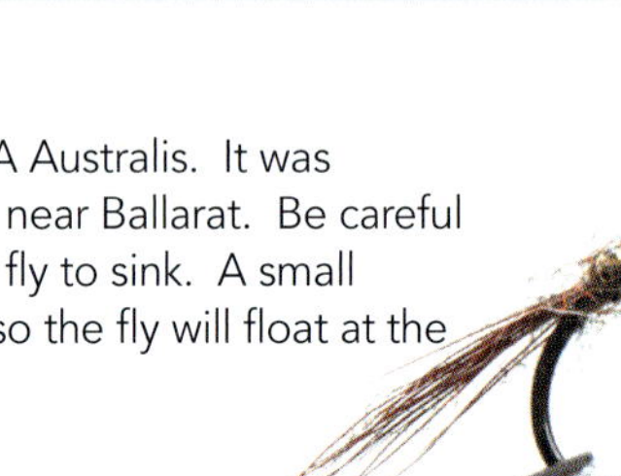

Hook	#14 L/S down eye
Tail	Fiery Brown hackle fibres tied short
Body	Natural raw dark brown wool
Wing case	Dark brown Etha foam strip

PEACOCK AND BROWN EMERGER

This fly comes from Australian competitive fly angler Simon Taylor.

Hook	#12 caddis bend
Tail	Brown hackle
Body	Brown seal fur
Rib	Copper pot scrubber
Thorax	Peacock herl
Post	Hi-Viz
Hackle	Brown cock

SHAVING BRUSH

Congratulations to David Dodd of Ballarat for creating this very successful and extremely popular fly. I remember well tying one on for Mervyn Hughes, (yes, the cricketer) at Hepburn Lagoon in Victoria, he then went on and landed at least a dozen nice rainbows on it. Colours can be varied to suit local mayflies. It works best for me when pulled across the surface to create a wake. (It is also an effective dry fly when grasshoppers are about.)

Hook	#10-14
Tail	Black cock hackle fibres
Body	Dark dubbing mix
Rib	Copper wire
Wing	Deer hair. Angle it steeply
Head	A ball of dubbing to flair out the wing

SILVER MARCH BROWN

Another traditional wet pattern used as an optional dropper fly for 'loch style' fishing.

Hook	#10-14
Tail	Brown partridge
Body	Flat silver tinsel ribbed with silver oval or wire
Wing	Hen pheasant wing slips
Hackle	Brown partridge

UPSIDE-DOWN EMERGER

Thanks to Geoff Hall of the Goulburn Valley Fly Fishing Centre for this fly. Geoff's notation is: "*This fly has been made possible by the exploratory work of Paul Zumica who first showed me how to use a swimming nymph hook to construct an emerger. All new flies are revolutionary, but some are also revolutionary in approach and this fly fills both criteria*". A pattern also recommended by Rod Barford. Geoff also ties it in other colours. It is a fly that works for him.

Hook	#12-16 L/S swimming nymph hook
Tail	Cock hackle tied short
Body	Seal fur or other dubbing ribbed with fine copper wire
Thorax	As for the body
Wing case	Dark turkey
Legs	Elk hair whisks tied in above the thorax and under the wing
Wing	Paired turkey or brown partridge wing slips
Hackle	Tied parachute around the wing

WALLABY NO HACKLE

Rod Barford. After completion the thorax is lightly teased out for legs.

Hook	#12 dry fly
Tail	Cochybondhu hackle fibres
Body	Wallaby underfur
Rib	Fine gold wire
Wing	Wallaby fur with guard hairs removed
Thorax	Wallaby underfur

MAYFLY SPINNERS

AUSTRALIS SPINNER

Andrew Overton.

Hook	#14
Tail	Black hackle
Body	Red Macaw
Rib	Fine gold wire
Hackle	Furnace cock

MARCH BROWN PALMER

This is also a top dropper fly tied and supplied by master fly tier David Dodd from Ballarat. David's flies are very exact and of the highest standard.

Hook	TMC #12-14
Tail	Yellow wool tag
Body	Dubbed 75% hares ear fur and 25% orange seal fur
Rib	Fine gold wire
Palmer	Furnace hackle with 2 turns of brown partridge at the front

BLACK SPINNER

Unknown origin, but a very successful old fly pattern. It can be winged with natural black hen wing strips.

Hook	#12
Tail	Black cock hackle fibres tied long
Body	Black tying silk
Rib	Fine silver wire
Hackle	Black cock

COCKY SPINNER

Credited to the late Tasmanian, Major W.B. Howlett. (It is a fly I have fished a lot). The hackles can be 'figure eighted' underneath to create a spent spinner.

Hook	#12
Tail	3 strands natural red cock hackle
Body	2 strands red macaw tail feather
Rib	Gold wire
Hackle	One each of natural red and grizzle

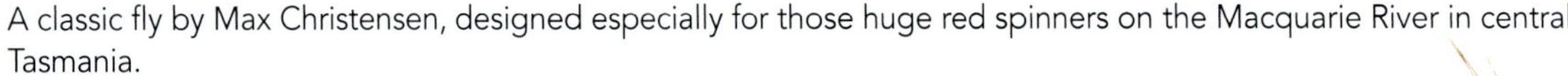

MACQUARIE RED SPINNER

A classic fly by Max Christensen, designed especially for those huge red spinners on the Macquarie River in central Tasmania.

Hook	#12 L/S up-eye
Tail	Three stiff red cock hackle fibres
Body	Well waxed orange thread
Rib	Fine copper wire
Palmer	A small natural red cock hackle
Thorax	Bronze peacock herl
Hackle	One each of red and Cree
Head	Black thread

ORANGE QUILL

A Noel Jetson fly.

Hook	#12 down eye
Thread	Hot orange
Tail	Hot orange dyed hackle fibres
Body	Stripped quill from a large dyed orange hackle feather
Hackle	Light red cock

ORANGE SPINNER

A Keith Draper pattern from New Zealand.

Hook	#12-14
Thread	Orange
Tail	Ginger cock hackle fibres
Body	Orange wool
Rib	Fine gold wire
Hackle	Ginger cock

PARACHUTE SPENT SPINNER

Variations of colour will suit lots of different mayfly colourations.

Hook	#12-14
Tail	Black hackle fibres
Body	Black floss
Rib	Red copper wire
Post	Hi-Viz
Hackle	Black cock

RED SPINNER

Hook	#12-14
Tail	Long stiff black hackle fibres or micro fibbets
Body	Reddish orange Floss
Rib	Fine gold wire
Hackle	Red cock

SHERRY SPINNER

Yet another English fly, this time from the legendary G.E.M Skues. The original pattern had the body made from Hare's Ear fur but floss is much easier to use.

Hook #14-16
Tail Reddish tipped pheasant tail fibres
Body Orange floss
Wings Blue dun hackle points tied spent
Hackle Light ginger cock

SMALL SPENT BLACK SPINNER

Jan spencer (Fly Bird) contributed this classic fly.

Hook #14
Tail Long black micro fibbets
Body Black tread
Rib Fine silver tinsel
Wings Sparse Hi-Viz tied flat
Hackle Black cock clipped underneath

SPENT CAENID SPINNER

Hook #14 - 18
Tail Black hackle fibres tied split
Body Black floss
Wings Hi-Viz tied flat
Thorax Dubbed white rabbit fur

SPENT ORANGE SPINNER

Tied by Tasmanian, Jan Spencer. This fly mimics the A. Australis imago. The plastic body gives the fly a very attractive glow. A spent version of this fly would need Hi-Viz wings tied flat and the hackle trimmed off at the bottom or figure eighted.

Hook #10-12
Tail Long orange microfibbets
Body Orange plastic strip over black thread
Hackle Medium red

BLACK MUDDLER MINNOW

Hook	#6-10
Tail	Black squirrel
Body	Silver tinsel
Wing	Black crow
Head	Dyed black deer hair

MUDDLER MINNOW

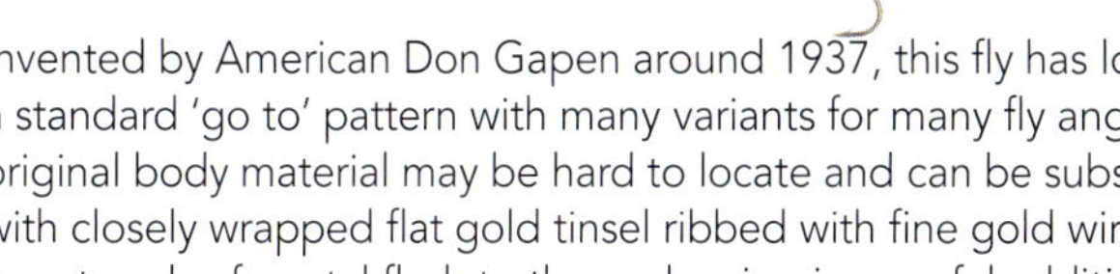

Invented by American Don Gapen around 1937, this fly has long been a standard 'go to' pattern with many variants for many fly anglers. The original body material may be hard to locate and can be substituted with closely wrapped flat gold tinsel ribbed with fine gold wire. A few strands of crystal flash to the underwing is a useful addition. This fly can be fished dry and is a good option when Bogong moths or grasshoppers are around. It can also be used as a pulling fly for smelting fish.

Hook	#4-12
Tail	Mottled turkey
Body	Gold diamond braid
Underwing	Grey squirrel
Wing	Mottled turkey
Collar	Grey deer hair
Head	As above

JINDY MUDDLER

Provided by the late Ty Smith, who was a guide at Jindabyne for some years until his death. He fished the fly on a short leader with slow twitches.

Hook	#6-8
Underbody	Lead wire
Body	Gold twist
Underwing	Dyed purple mallard breast feather
Over-wing	Black marabou
Head	Black deer hair spun muddler style
Collar	As above

OLIVE CRYSTAL MUDDLER

Hook	#6-10 L/S
Body	Green Crystal Flash or diamond braid
Wing	Grey squirrel, mottled turkey and pearl crystal flash
Collar	Bright red wool or dubbing
Head	Dyed olive deer hair

NYMPHS

BELLY DANCER

Made and designed by Alan Barber who owns and runs "Tiewell", in Katoomba NSW, he supplies all sorts of amazing hooks and fly tying materials for anglers. Look out for his products in your preferred tackle store. The fly is tied on a caddis grub hook. I have chosen not to give specific material but directly quote Alan's notes:

'A simple nymph weighted with a bead at the centre. The location of the bead ensures that the fly rides point up. It can be tied with various dubbings such a super possum or hare's ear. Because there is no tail the fly can be tied in quite large sizes without looking too big in the water, although sizes 14-16 are the most popular'.

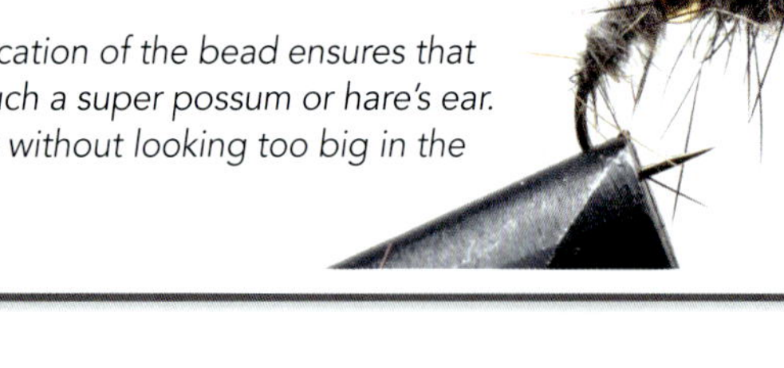

BIDGEE STONEFLY NYMPH

A contribution from Neil Charter of Bombala. He advises this fly works well in the Murrumbidgee and holds sentimental value for him as, with it, he won the 1996 NSW Fly Fishing Championships. He only uses it if dry flies aren't being taken.

Hook	#10
Tail	Black goose biot
Rib	Fine gold tinsel over full length
Body	Black seal fur
Wingcase	Gold Flashback

BLACK AND PEACOCK

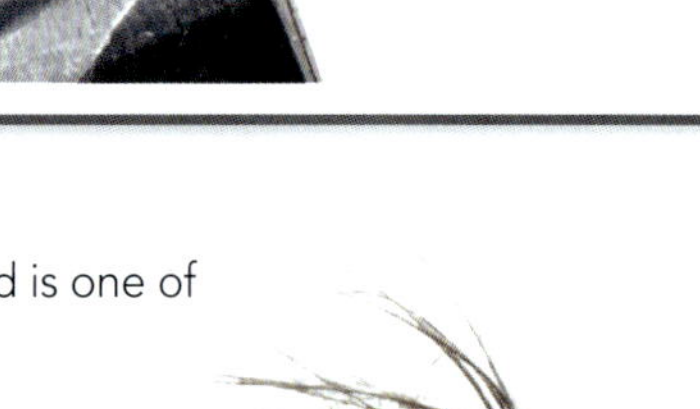

This small fly is a good representation of water snails or small black beetles, and is one of the late Noel Jetsons contributions.

Hook	#12-16
Body	Bronze peacock herl
Hackle	One turn of natural black hen

BLACK NYMPH

From Copielle Roland, a Belgian I met at the 1996 World Championships. Note: this is a bulky fly.

Hook	#8-12
Weight	Lead wire
Tag	Red floss
Tail	Black
Body	Black seal fur
Rib	Silver oval tinsel
Thorax	Black dubbing with spectra flash
Head	Red varnish

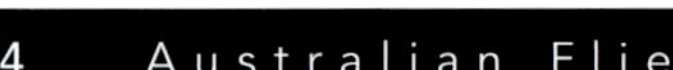

BLACK AND RED NYMPH

I acquired this fly from an angler I met at a Melbourne boat show who like me, liked fishing Malmsbury Reservoir in the days when it was kept full and was a quality trout fishery. I caught a number of fish on it as well. Like most effective flies, it is simple.

Hook	#10-12
Tail	Black hackle fibres
Body	Rear half red chenille, front half black chenille
Hackle	Black hen

BLACK AND YELLOW

A nymph I like for lake fishing. Use a slow retrieve.

Hook	#8-12
Tail	Black hackle
Body	Thinly dubbed yellow seal fur. Green and orange are good too
Hackle	Black hen

BLOCKHEAD NYMPH

This entry was supplied by my life-long friend, the late Marty Rogers, and being his own attempt at fly tying. It was named after Marty by his son Zac, because of the ungainly silk head. I have no idea of its success or otherwise. I still smile at the humour expressed in the name. It is included for interest sake. Marty was a well-known and iconic entity at the Compleat Angler in Melbourne for some decades.

Hook	#10
Tail	Rhode Island Red hackle fibres
Body	Brown seal fur
Rib	Gold wire
Head	Black thread very bulky

BOURKE'S NYMPH

The late Bill Bourke described it as "that nymph". He made it famous and was renowned as a local angler in his home town of Alexandra, Victoria.

Hook	#12 L/S
Tail	Blue dun cock
Underbody	Fine lead wire
Body	Royal purple seals fur
Palmer	Blue dun tied in by point and wound forward
Throat	Whisks blue dun

BROWN AND SILVER NYMPH 

This fly is a flashback version of a standard brown seal fur nymph.

Hook #10-12
Tail Brown hackle fibres
Body Brown seal fur
Rib Fine copper pot scrubber
Wing case Wide silver tinsel

CASUAL DRESS NYMPH 

This fly came from American Polly Rosborough. I found it in Poul Jorgensen's book "Modern Trout Flies".

Hook # 10 or 12 L/S 12 is also an option
Tail Mole fur
Body Dubbed mole fur
Hackle Flared mole fur
Head Black ostrich herl

COLOBURISCUS NYMPH 

A favoured nymph from Ross Lavis. This is the larvae of the renowned Kosciuszko Dun.

Hook #10-12 L/S
Underbody Flattened lead wire
Body Dark brown ostrich herl clipped top and bottom
Rib Fine copper pot scrubber or copper wire
Thorax Dubbed dark hare's ear
Wing case Wide Lava Lace

COPPER JOHN 

Invented in the 1990's by John Barr of Boulder, Colorado, who works as a fly developer for Umpqua. The fly went through a series of changes until it emerged in its present form. It sinks quickly, works a treat and has become universally known and fished with regular success. In larger sizes it can represent a caddis, or it is readily taken as a midge when tied much smaller. Variants have brass, green, red or even pink wire.

Hook #10-18 X/l or XX/L
Tail Goose biots
Underbody Lead wire to around mid-shank, then over-bound with thread to form an even taper.
Body Copper wire tapered up to the thorax
Legs Hen hackle.
Thorax Peacock herl
Wingcase "Thin Skin" or dark turkey with a strip of holographic tinsel over the top. After completion a coat of epoxy is applied to the wing case. It may need two coats if turkey is used as the first will soak in
Head Gold brass bead

DOUBLE HACKLED BEAD HEAD

Rob Flower. I developed this fly out of a desire to create a heavy fly with maximum movement. This is not a handsome fly by any means. I have never seen a drowned insect that looked anything but dishevelled. This fly fulfils that role well. I tie it in black, brown, green, hare's ear, prince and as a grasshopper. For the 'prince' version I add white goose biots as wings.

Hook	#10-14
Underbody	Lead wire
Tail	Cock hackle or goose biots
Body	Seals fur
Rib	Copper wire or narrow pot scrubber
Bead	Tungsten
Hackle	Cock hackle at back and front of the bead

FOAM EMERGER

Provided by Tasmanian John O'Halloran. He uses it on Tasmanian Highland Lakes during dun hatches.

Hook	#12
Tail	Fiery brown hackle fibres
Body	Dubbed brown seal fur
Rib	Fine copper wire
Wing	Tan coloured closed cell foam trimmed to shape
Thorax	As for body
Hackle	Fiery brown tied parachute

FISH RIVER NYMPHS 1 & 2

Favoured weapons of guide Jeff Brown of Emu Plains NSW. There are two versions of this fly, the second of which slims the body down from dubbed fur to a layer of brown tying thread and a thorax of peacock herl. He fishes these both as traditional nymphs and also under a dry fly indicator.

Hook	#12
Tail	Black of dark brown cock hackle.
Body	Fly #1 is dubbed brown possum fur tied sparse and scruffy Fly #2 use tying thread
Rib	Fine copper wire
Thorax	As for the body
Head	A small copper bead

GP NYMPH

John Orr from Tasmania kindly gave me this fly, and he teases out the thorax fur for legs. I have no knowledge of what 'GP' stands for. John also says that most fly tier's make the tails of nymphs too long. The standard length for tails is the same as the hook shank, but John prefers them to be only half that length. Blends of seal fur can vary to suit. Give it a try.

Hook	#10-12
Tail	Short cock hackle
Body	A blend of 50% brown, 10% black, 20% red, 10% olive green and 10% lime seals fur
Rib	Copper wire
Thorax	Dubbed blend of seal fur as above
Wing Case	Raffia or similar

GOLD RIBBED HARES EAR NYMPH 

A good performer in stillwaters around weed beds. Weight it with lead wire if required.

Hook	#12-16
Tail	Ginger hackle
Body	Dubbed hares ear fur
Rib	Fine gold wire
Wing case	Grey duck quill
Thorax	As for body

GREYBEARD 

A fly credited to John Potts a former member of Northern Suburbs Fly Fishers in Melbnourne. A good performer in stillwaters around weed beds. Weight it with lead wire if required.

Hook	#6-8 L/S
Tail	Golden Pheasant tippets
Body	Rear half Yellow floss or polythene wrap, front half Green seal fur well picked out
Hackle	Short grizzle to front half only
Wing case	Tan poly string or natural raffia

HEPBURN NYMPH 

This fly came to me as a fluke. Having landed a good rainbow on a blue chironomid nymph I discovered this fly also stuck in corner of its jaw. I tied some more and have caught a few fish on it at that same lake. Obviously, a caddis imitation.

Hook	#10
Bead	White glass bead put on first
Tail	Red wool with 2 strands of pearl crystal flash
Body	Short peacock ice chenille

JINDABYNE NYMPH 

An original pattern from Dalton Neville of the ACT, and supplied by Bill Lade. This is a larger than normal nymph.

Hook	#6-8
Tail	Golden Pheasant tippets
Body	Black angora or wool
Rib	Flat copper wire
Wing	Brown hackle tied short
Thorax	Dubbed red and white seal fur
Antennae	Brown hackle points

JOES NYMPH

As supplied by Keith McPherson. This is a bulky fly. Keith made no mention of fishing methods.

Hook	6-8 L/S
Tail	Brown hackle fibres
Body	Brown seal fur ribbed with copper wire
Thorax	As for body
Hackle	Brown cock sloped backwards
Head	Well varnished thread

LASER NYMPH

I have used this fly with great success and given it to friends who often ask for more, which says a lot. Tied weighted or as a beadhead and fished in streams in fast broken water it is always worth a try. I won a session on the Kiewa River near Mt. Beauty with this fly in rising water.

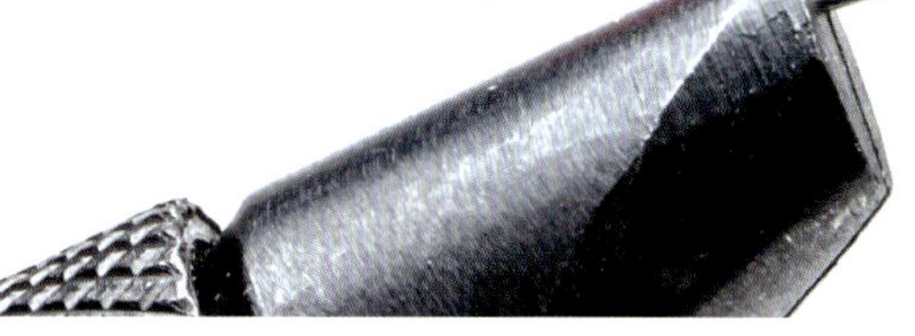

Hook	#10-16
Tail	Red cock hackle fibres
Body	Peacock laser lights dubbing
Rib	A single strand of bright yellow floss
Thorax	Peacock laser dubbing
Bead	Gold or copper tungsten is optional

LIFEJACKET NYMPH

Designed by Maj. Gen. Frank Hickling to imitate stillborn mayfly emergers stuck in the surface film of water. Stillborn's are particular favourites when trout are mopping up mayflies during hatching events.

Hook	#12
Tail	Darkish brown partridge
Body	Brown seal fur or colour to suit
Rib	Gold tinsel
Lifejacket	A loop of closed cell foam
Thorax	As for body
Hackle	Brown or grizzle tied in before the thorax

LITTLE NYMPH

Chris Hole angler, artist and author of "Heaven on a Stick" gave me this pattern. I have seen some huge fish taken in the Eucumbene River at the end of the angling season on this fly, and even had a loan of one 'brute' myself until it saw me and took off, never to be seen again.

Hook	#12-16 long shank
Tail	Golden Pheasant tippet
Body	Black seal fur
Rib	Fine gold wire
Wing case	Black crow
Hackle	One turn of black hen
Head	Black varnish

MARCH BROWN NYMPH

Rob Flower. I tied this fly as a swimming nymph for pre-hatch fishing in Victoria's Western Lakes where these insects are common. It is well weighted, has a heavily varnished red head to signify the weight and the hook shank has been hand bent upward at the thorax. Standard down eye hooks will not swim level when retrieved, but applying this bend ensures they do. I have caught lots of fish on it especially in Lake Wendouree as a point fly.

Hook	#12 L/S
Tail	Cock pheasant centre tail tips showing red and tied short
Body	Cock pheasant centre tail
Rib	Fine copper wire wound on in opposite direction to the body material.
Wing case	Cock pheasant centre tail
Thorax	Peacock laser-light dubbing
Hackle	One turn of brown hen

MONTANA NYMPH

Wow, what a killing fly. Variations aplenty too, and that is always a good indication of the value of a fly pattern. This fly bears a close resemblance to the stonefly nymphs so common in Montana and other parts of the USA. Being specialised to a species the surprise is its adaption worldwide with stunning success. The originator is unknown, developing over time.

Hook	#10-12
Tail	Black hackle fibres
Body	Black chenille ribbed with silver tinsel
Wing case	Two strands of black chenille
Thorax	Yellow or lime green chenille
Hackle	Soft black cock palmered through the thorax

MONTANA NYMPH VARIANT

Hook	#10
Underbody	Fine lead wire
Tail	Dark brown hackle fibres
Body	Black chenille ribbed with silver tinsel
Wing case	Two strands of black chenille
Thorax	Yellow or lime green chenille
Hackle	Soft black cock palmered over thorax

MONTANA STONE

Hook	#10-12 XX/L shank
Tail	Divided black goose biots
Underbody	Lead wire
Abdomen	Black chenille
Thorax	Yellow chenille
Legs	Thee winds of black hackle over the thorax
Wing case	Black chenille

EUCUMBENE MONTANA

Hook	#10-12 XXL/S
Underbody	Lead wire (optional)
Tail	Black hen Hackle fibres
Body	Very thin black chenille
Thorax	Thin olive chenille ribbed with red hen hackle
Wing case	Green peacock sword

BEAD HEAD MONTANA

The same as above with the addition of a brass or tungsten bead. A change of thorax to fluoro lime green or chartreuse is a useful variation. Use the same 'tie' as for a Montana nymph using a gold brass or tungsten bead. Lead wire to the shank will make it even heavier for a quick sink rate.

MUSKRAT BEAD-HEAD

A fly supplied by Del Bruce of Ajax, Ontario, a member of the Canadian fly fishing team.

Hook	#12
Tail	Muskrat or fox
Rib	Gold wire
Body	Dubbed muskrat or fox
Collar	As above
Head	Brass bead

NYMBEET

Another famous Tasmanian fly, this time from Stuart Napier. A variant uses thin black chenille for the body, and it is ribbed with narrow copper pot scrubber.

Hook	#10-12
Tail	Natural black hackle fibres
Wing case	Strip of black crow doubled over
Underbody	Black floss
Body	Clear plastic pot scrubber that is now very hard to source, or alternatively Lava Lace
Hackle	Soft natural black cock

PERSUADER NYMPH

From Englishman John Goddard, who is better known for his caddis flies.

Hook	#8 L/S.
Body	White Ostrich herl
Rib	Silver oval tinsel
Thorax	Dubbed orange seal fur
Wing Case	Dark turkey

PHEASANT TAIL NYMPH

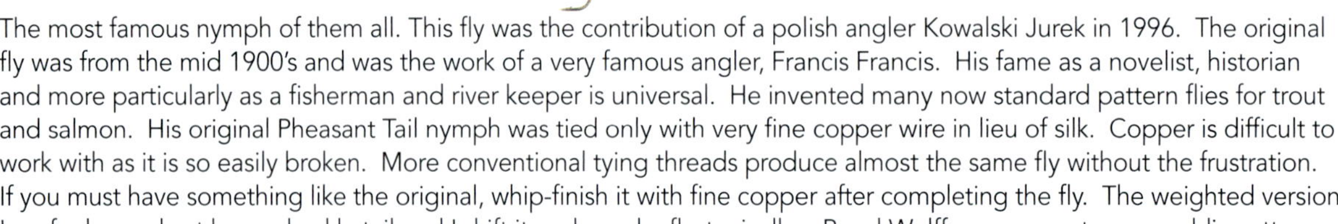

The most famous nymph of them all. This fly was the contribution of a polish angler Kowalski Jurek in 1996. The original fly was from the mid 1900's and was the work of a very famous angler, Francis Francis. His fame as a novelist, historian and more particularly as a fisherman and river keeper is universal. He invented many now standard pattern flies for trout and salmon. His original Pheasant Tail nymph was tied only with very fine copper wire in lieu of silk. Copper is difficult to work with as it is so easily broken. More conventional tying threads produce almost the same fly without the frustration. If you must have something like the original, whip-finish it with fine copper after completing the fly. The weighted version I prefer has a short brown hackle tail and I drift it under a dry fly, typically a Royal Wulff, or an easy to see caddis pattern. As a tail, Pheasant tail fibres are brittle and easily broken off. Substitute it with red/brown hackle.

Hook	#14-16
Underbody	Copper wire
Wing case	Pheasant tail fibres
Tail	Pheasant tail fibres
Body	Wrapped Pheasant tail fibres
Rib	Fine copper wire wound in opposite direction to body material

PHILBRICK NYMPH

Original tie of John Philbrick supplied to me by Jim Harmon of AFN, and a personal favourite of Jim Allen. The feature of this fly is the long slim profile.

Hook	#10-16 X/L shank
Tail	Dark red hackle fibres
Body	Dubbed blended seal fur, dark brown, red, black yellow and olive
Rib	Fine copper wire

PRINCE

An all-round favourite in a standard nymph, weighted or as a bead-head.

Hook	#8-14 L/S
Tail	Dark brown goose biots
Weight	Lead wire or bead heads are optional
Body	Bronze peacock herl
Rib	Fine gold oval tinsel
Legs	Two turns of brown hen hackle
Wings	White goose biots

RIPPLE NYMPH 

Also known as a 'riffle nymph' it was invented in 1969 by Gerd Benecke. His notation says "the reason for the long throat hackle was to turn the fly upside down, this gives the fly a life like action, imparting movement when retrieved in short pulls. This is most effective in weedy lakes and helps to avoid snagging". Gerd tied this fly in brown, black, burnt orange, olive and hare's ear. Note: the beard is meant to be at least as long as the full length of the hook.

Hook	#10-14
Tail	Hackle fibres
Body	Dubbed black seal fur
Wing case	Crow or hen wing feather
Rib	Red wire
Thorax	Seal fur
Beard	Stiff black cock hackle tied long

TEDS STONE FLY

Hook	#10-12 XX/L.
Tail	Two brown goose biots, short and split
Abdomen	Brown chenille
Thorax	Orange chenille ribbed with dark brown hackle
Wing Case	Brown chenille

TOM JONES 

The invention of John Lanchester from Woodend, Victoria. Despite several requests he declined to provide his original tying, but from what I know this is fairly close. It is best fished with a very slow 'figure 8' retrieve. Does it resemble a stick caddis or a baby red fin?

Hook	#8-10
Tail	Black hackle fibres
Body	Sparsely dubbed dyed green cotton wool
Wings	Two sparse clumps of dyed green wallaby fur with black tips
	One is tied in about halfway, and the other at the head
Head	Well defined black varnish

TOM JONES BEAD HEAD 

A variant of the original likened to helter smelter and the BMS Special and credited to John Rumpf.

Tail	Black hackle fibres
Body	Sparsely dubbed dyed green cotton wool
Wings	Two sparse clumps of dyed green wallaby fur with black tips
	One is tied in about halfway, and the other at the head
Head	A yellow glass bead over well-defined black varnish

RUMPF'S GREY TOM

Another good fly from renowned angler John Rumpf.

Hook	#10-12L/S
Tail	Black squirrel tail
Butt	Burnt orange seal fur
Body	Dubbed squirrel under fur
Wing	Squirrel tail tied in two tufts, Tom Jones style

ORANGE TOM

Source unknown.

Hook	#10-12
Tail	Black hackle fibres
Body	Sparsely dubbed orange seal fur
Rib	Flat gold tinsel
Wing	Orange rabbit in two clumps short and sparse
Head	Well defined black varnish

PEARL TOM

Another variant on the 'Tom Jones' that changes its character completely.

Hook	#6-8
Tail	Grey or red Hackle fibres
Body	Halved both of pearl tinsel
Wings	Both of pale olive fur

ZUG BUG

Originated by American, Cliff Zug.

Hook	#10-16 X/L shank
Tail	Three peacock sword feathers
Body	Peacock herl
Rib	Oval silver tinsel
Legs	Brown Hackle
Wingcase	Folded mallard flank strip

007 NYMPH

For many years a well-kept secret pattern by central Tasmanian guide Ken Orr, who runs 'Orrsome tours'. The fly is fished static about 10cm under a dry fly. He also has a 008 but I have not been able to locate that pattern.

Hook	#12
Tail	Hot orange wool
Body	Black seals fur
Rib	Thin blue tinsel or wire
Wingcase	Crow

SCUD

Scuds, also known as Gamarus, are a freshwater amphipod (crustacean) occurring in slow running rivers and lakes. They are readily consumed by trout and are a nutrient rich staple food source especially to juvenile fish. Gamarus flies are a specialty of anglers in middle Europe but largely ignored here. They are especially good for 'tailing fish' and can be fished static in a few inches of water by casting them near to, and in front of a tailing fish, and then waiting for the trout to find it. Watch a well-greased leader for the slightest movement. Tailing fish are a sure sign that these animals are being targeted.

BEAD THING #1

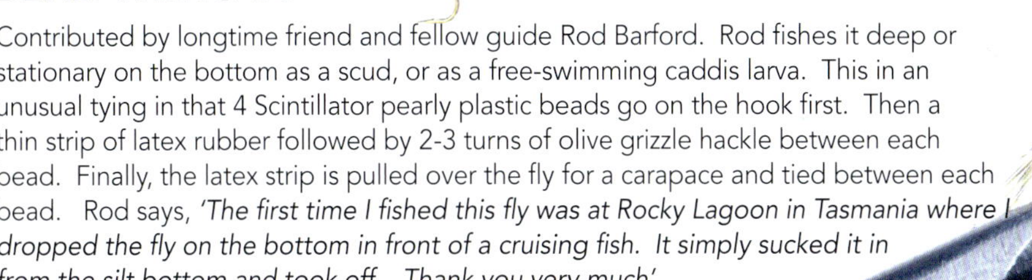

Contributed by longtime friend and fellow guide Rod Barford. Rod fishes it deep or stationary on the bottom as a scud, or as a free-swimming caddis larva. This in an unusual tying in that 4 Scintillator pearly plastic beads go on the hook first. Then a thin strip of latex rubber followed by 2-3 turns of olive grizzle hackle between each bead. Finally, the latex strip is pulled over the fly for a carapace and tied between each bead. Rod says, *'The first time I fished this fly was at Rocky Lagoon in Tasmania where I dropped the fly on the bottom in front of a cruising fish. It simply sucked it in from the silt bottom and took off. Thank you very much'.*

BEAD THING #2

Is the same as version 1 but with black ostrich herl between each bead.

Hook	#12 caddis bend
Body	Pearly plastic beads
Hackle	Olive grizzle
Back	Latex rubber tied in between each bead

CHOMPER

An English take on the scud. It can be tied in various colours and the ribbing is optional.

Hook	#12-14 caddis bend
Underbody	Lead wire optional
Carapace	Raffia or clear scud back
Body	Grey ostrich herl
Thorax	Light green Seal fur
Rib	3kg monofilament

GAMARUS

This fly was supplied by a Polish angler Kruzecki Marek, where gamarus (scud) are often a 'first choice' fly in a team of nymphs. These flies come in a variety of often bright colours, tied on heavy caddis bend hooks.

Hook #12-14 caddis bend
Tail A few strands of olive cock hackle tied short
Back Plastic strip or scud-back
Rib 6lb brown monofilament
Body Olive seals fur that is teased out
Head Trimmed plastic
Feelers Olive hackle

FANTAS GAMARUS

Another European tying from Pavel Machan who was a member of the Czech world team in 1996.

Hook #8 heavy caddis grub
Back Sparkly pearl plastic
Body First 2/3 white seal, last 1/3 yellow seal fur picked out
Rib 3kg brown monofilament

TANDEM FLIES

An English idea that I have tried here in Australia with success. Based on the 'red tag' it can be tied on a very long shank hook, or two flies joined with heavy nylon. Either way is suitable. If using nylon one size smaller sized fly at back seems best. There are a number of wet flies that are suitable for this treatment. The rabbit is a fly that I used in Alaska for various large salmon species that are plentiful there. These flies were tied on 2/0 low-water salmon hooks. White, purple and black or black and red were popular. I have caught large trout here on the red and black at the end of the season.

WORM FLY #1 - RED TAG

Two wet red tag flies joined with 15kg mono well glued in position.

Hook XXXL shank #12
Tag Red wool
Body Peacock herl
Hackle Brown

WORM FLY #2 - RED AND BLACK MATUKA

The same idea as the red tag worm fly above but with two joined matuka flies using nylon to join them. If you are concerned about two full barbed hooks simply cut the front one off at the start of the hook bend.

Hook # 8 at front and #10 for the rear
Body Red wool or seal fur. Seal fur looks better
Rib Fine flat silver tinsel
Wing Two pairs of black hen saddle back to back
Eyes Jungle cock
Flash A single strand of pearl Crystal Flash down both sides of both tails

WORM FLY ALEXANDRA

Hook	#6-12
Tail	Red ibis or dyed red duck quill
Body	Flat silver tinsel
Rib	Sliver wire
Wing	Peacock sword
Hackle	Black hen
Flanks	Originally jungle-cock but now most often red duck quill

RABBIT

Tie the rear hook first. Firmly tie on the joiner line leaving it long at the rear and doubling it over. Super glue it, then proceed with the rest of the rear fly. When the body is complete, pierce a length of rabbit zonker strip near the end, thread the rear hook through the hole and proceed to the front hook. On the front hook tie in the joiner leaving it long at the front and doubling it over, before gluing. Lead wire can be added to aid sinking in fast or deep water. This is a big fly so slow down your casting action. Lead wire and a cone head is the Alaskan standard to get the fly down deep. I have had some big fish on this fly in lakes at season's end when fish congregate at river mouths pre-spawning.

Rear hook	#6
Joiner	Two strands of 40kg braid stained with black marker
Body	Red wool
Rib	Silver oval tinsel
Head	Well varnished thread
Front hook	#4
Body	Red wool
Rib	Silver oval tinsel
Wing	Black zonker strip ribbed down matuka style
Throat	A clump of red Rabbit fur
Head	Well varnished thread

WET FLIES

ALEXANDRA

A traditional Scottish pattern circa 1860, it was also known as 'lady of the lake'. So successful it is reported to have been outlawed in some Scottish waters. Best fished to waltz time, i.e. slow, slow, quick-quick, slow. A retrieve well worth remembering for all sorts of other flies. This is another fly that is well suited to making as a tandem fly (see WORM FLIES). In Australia it is often used as a night-time fly to represent emerging mudeyes, and as such is made larger than in the UK where it's usual to see it in #10-12.

Hook	#6-12
Tail	Red ibis or dyed red duck quill
Body	Flat silver tinsel
Rib	Sliver wire
Wing	Peacock sword
Hackle	Black hen
Flanks	Originally jungle-cock but now most often red duck quill

BAG FLY

This fly was invented by George Heller around 1940 and had a great reputation in the Eildon area of Victoria, and elsewhere as a smelt pattern. There were two versions of this fly but the one with the wing tied down at the tail seems to have been lost with the passage of time

Hook	#6-10
Tail	Black cock
Body	Flat gold tinsel
Throat	Black hackle fibres
Wing	Hessian from a sugar or wheat bag
Overwing	Long orange hackle fibres

BARBARIAN

Another of my own variations, probably not original.

Hook	#10-14
Tail	Black cock hackle
Body	Red wool
Wings	Soft black rabbit fur

BECK'S CAT FLY

Bill Beck's most famous creation. This fly has an enviable reputation. In his early days before creating the cat pattern, the "Wigram's Robin" was a favourite of Bill's at places like Little Pine Lagoon where he was known for his faster than normal retrieve technique. Feral cat fur is highly recommended, kill plenty till you get one the right colour.

Hook	#6-8
Tail	Golden Pheasant tippets
Body	Dubbed muddy yellow seal fur
Wing	Strip of brown cat or seal fur tied yeti style
Rib	Thin silver tinsel

BECK'S PRINCESS

Bill Beck a Tasmanian angler with a huge reputation, created this fly. The pattern here is courtesy of Malcolm Crosse.

Hook	#6-10
Tag	Hot orange wool
Body	Black chenille
Rib	Silver tinsel wrap
Wing	Black musquash

BLACK CAT

Paul Brabham from Bathurst Fly Fishers supplied this fly. If you can't murder your neighbour's 'moggy' or 'score' a feral one, rabbit can be used. Feral cats are recommended. This is a bulky fly designed to push some water.

Hook	#8-10
Weight	Fine lead wire
Tail	Red wool (optional)
Body	Yellow or red chenille
Wings	Bunches of black cat fur in 2 halves, first bunch halfway along, and second bunch at head Note: the wings are rather thick so that they will form a mudeye shape when wet
Head	Black chenille or ostrich

BLACK CENTIPEDE

Terry Sheppard created this fly in 1995 for use on the Eildon Pondage where black centipedes or more likely millipedes were falling off the steep spillway wall and being taken by trout.

Hook	#8-10 wide gape
Body	Small soft plastic or glass balls cemented in position

BLACK AND PEACOCK SPIDER

How often do we see strands of spider web blowing in the breeze? This is the way spiderlings spread out from their place of birth. This little fly is a favourite of my regular fishing mate Ralph Nagle and I on lakes. In autumn or winter, simple to tie and can be very effective.

Hook	#14-16
Thread	Black
Body	First half black thread
Thorax	Peacock herl
Hackle	Two turns of black cock

BLACK PHANTOM

Unknown. A New Zealand fly for night fishing.

Hook	#6-8
Tail	Black squirrel
Body	Black wool or chenille
Rib	Silver oval tinsel
Wings	Black Pukeko feather tied killer style
Cheeks	Jungle cock eyes (optional)

BLACK PHANTOM (AUSSIE STYLE) 

I suspect that this fly was developed by Norm King, a fantastic nighttime fisher. In the past when Lake Modewarre was producing big rainbows, I know he was a regular there and this type of innovation is just his style. The idea of the pearl body is for it to glow thru the wing.

Hook	#6-8
Body	Pearl Lureflash over heavy white thread with several coats of clear Softex or pearl nail polish.
Wings	Back to back black hen hackle or cock spade feathers, semi-transparent is best
Cheeks	Jungle cock

BLARNEY SMELT 

As used by Pat O'Keefe of Blarney Lodge, New Zealand.

Hook	#6-8
Tail	Dyed black squirrel
Body	Green seal fur well teased out
Rib	Fine copper pot scrubber

BLEEDIN WET 

A Peter Coulson fly well suited as a middle dropper fly in a team of wets. I like the thought of a variant with golden pheasant toppings as the tail.

Hook	#10-14
Tail	Black hackle fibres
Body	Rear 1/3 red seals fur, front 2/3 black
Rib	Fine silver oval tinsel
Wing	Black hackle fibres
Hackle	Black hen
Cheeks	Jungle cock

BLOODY MARY 

A very famous fly indeed, created by legendary Tasmanian fly tier Max Christensen. Note the heavy hackle style. The pattern comes from Max Stokes little book "Tasmanian Trout Fly Patterns" and the fly given to me by "Macka" Brian McCullagh from Tasmania.

Hook	#8
Tag	Red marabou silk
Body	Red Lurex
Ribbing	Fine silver wire
Hackle	Poor quality palmered black hackle, the softer the better
Head	Black tying thread well varnished with a diamond of red lurex set in it on both sides
Note	The hackle is tied in at the tail end and wound forward, sparse at first with heavier hackle at the front and leaving space for the head. The hackle should also be tied to slope backward

BMS (BULLEN MERRI SPECIAL)

The late Murray Wilson designed this fly for use on Lake Bullen Merri in Victoria, but it is successful anywhere for smelting fish. In tying, the SLF is chopped into about 12-15mm lengths and given a good rub before dubbing it. After the fly is completed the SLF is teased out with Velcro. A medium to fast retrieve is best suited to this fly. It is thought to be a variant on Helter Skelter.

Hook	#10 X/L shank
Tail	Green SLF
Body	Dubbed green SLF
Rib	Flat gold tinsel
Head	Yellow or green glass bead
Overwing	long orange hackle fibres

BOOBY

This fly comes from a twice English trout master, Ian Marshall, who now resides in Australia. It is a very buoyant fly fished on the bottom with a fast sinking line and attached to a very short 50cm leader. The idea being that the fly rises vertical and hangs in the water just off the bottom. When given the occasional long slow pull on the line it makes the fly go down and then rise again, thus attracting attention. It is important to keep the rod tip touching the water and the line straight to detect takes. The fly can be made in a variety of colours. Yellow and black and yellow and green are the colours I know of, but others would be worth trying.

Hook	#6-10
Tail	Marabou
Butt	Fluoro yellow chenille
Body	Black chenille
Eyes	2 white styrene beads wrapped in nylon stocking (only one bead on smaller versions)

BRIAN'S ROUGHY

Invented by an old friend from school days, Brian Zschech who also lived in my street many years later.

Hook	#10 L/S
Tail	A pinch of green rabbit fur.
	Body and wing are formed together with alternate layers of purple wool and olive rabbit fur

BUTCHER

Originally known as 'Moons fly' and dating back to the 1830's, this was a very common fly along with the similar 'bloody butcher', both of which seem to have fallen out of favour. Perhaps due to the difficulty in finding the correct wing material and the cost of it if you do? The 'bloody' variety is the same as this fly but with a bright red hackle. In small sizes it can be fished slowly as a midge pupa, or larger ones as a baitfish fly.

Hook	#10-14
Tail	Red ibis or dyed duck quill
Body	Flat silver tinsel
Rib	Silver wire or oval
Hackle	Black or red hen
Wing	Blue mallard

CAT FLY

Another version of this now famous Tasmanian fly as supplied by former Australian representative Simon Taylor. He prefers a fast retrieve to imitate a stick caddis or may fly nymph.

Hook	#10 L/S
Tail	2 small hackle tips splayed outwards
Body	75% fiery brown and 25% claret seal fur mixed and ribbed with short brown hackle
Thorax	Same as body

CAT'S WHISKER

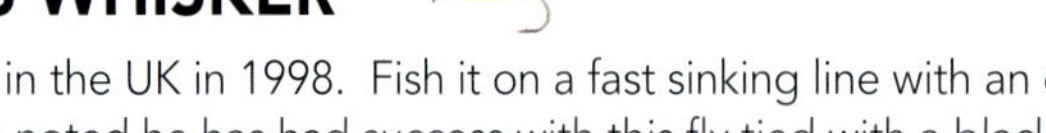

Created in the UK in 1998. Fish it on a fast sinking line with an erratic retrieve. Iain Barr also noted he has had success with this fly tied with a black marabou tail and wing. A daytime fly for bright conditions. This fly was given to me by Iain Barr who won the individual House of Hardy Championship.

Hook	#10
Tail	White marabou
Body	Fluoro yellow chenille
Rib	Oval silver tinsel
Wing	White marabou with a few 'cats' whiskers. Deer hair can be substituted
Eyes	Silver bead chain

CONNEMARA BLACK

Originally an Irish creation, it is another of Craig Coltman's recommendations fly for loch style fishing. To 'loch style' fly fishermen this fly is as famous as to the irish 'Guinness' and deservedly so.

Hook	#12
Tail	Golden pheasant toppings
Body	Dubbed black seal fur
Rib	Fine oval silver tinsel
Hackle	Black cock with blue jay or dyed grizzle at the front
Wing	Bronze mallard

CORIXIA (CROCHETED)

From Barry Whelan, a Ballarat Fly Fishers Club member.

Hook	#12-14
Underbody	White Hi-Viz over fine lead wire
Back	Brown raffia over the body leaving the white half underneath
Legs	Brown goose biots
Head	Fine brown dubbing

CORIXIA

Rod Barford.

Hook	#12-14 dry fly
Thread	Cream
Rib	Fine silver wire
Body	Light grey fluoro wool
Wingcase	Black/green Lureflash Shellback
Legs	Trimmed Grizzle hackle fibres

CORIXIA

A fly from my own fly-box, but of unknown origin.

Hook	#12-14
Wingcase	Mottled turkey
Body	Pale yellow wool
Rib	Fine silver wire
Legs	Red goose biots

BACKSWIMMER

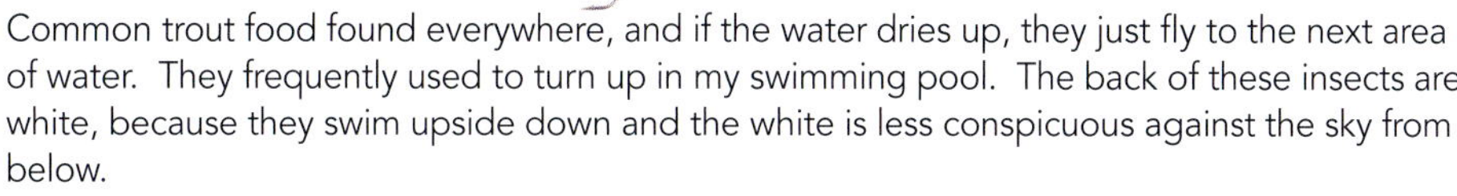

Common trout food found everywhere, and if the water dries up, they just fly to the next area of water. They frequently used to turn up in my swimming pool. The back of these insects are white, because they swim upside down and the white is less conspicuous against the sky from below.

Hook	#12
Back	White gift wrap ribbon tied below the body
Body	Light grey/green wool
Legs	Grey duck biots
Underbody	Hi-Viz

COTURNIX

A New Zealand 'killer' style fly I first tied when I liked the look of some rump feathers from brown quail that were supplied by my brother Victor. The Kiwi's call it a brown quail. It is in Keith Draper's book of New Zealand flies. It was successful fly as most 'killer' style flies are fair copies of the profile of large mud-eyes or small baitfish. The name derives from the Latin name for brown quail.

Hook	#6-8
Weight	Lead wire, optional
Tail	Barred squirrel or natural fox tail
Body	Red or Yellow wool or chenille tied in two sections
Wings	8 Quail rump feathers in two halves. Two pairs halfway along, then two more at the head, on both sides of the body

CRAIG'S NIGHTTIME

Originated by Mr. Eric Craig of Auckland, New Zealand in the 1930's. It is a standard pattern world-wide for day or night-time 'hatching' mudeye fishing. It also has many variants.

Hook	#4-10
Tag	Red wool
Body	Black wool or chenille
Rib	Thin silver oval tinsel
Wing	Blue Pukeko breast feathers, or substitute tied flat Pukeko are now protected and may be replaced by navy blue dyed hen feathers
Hackle	Black hen
Topping	The original pattern called for jungle cock eye feather on top of the wing. This is not easily found so it can be replaced by strands of dyed yellow cock hackle

CRAIG'S BLUE

This fly saved an otherwise fishless session for me in the last 10 minutes of a 'session' on Rocky Valley Dam by tripping up two fish.

Hook	#8
Tail	Orange wool
Body	Blue chenille
Rob	Flat silver tinsel
Wing	Blue Pukeko or substitute
Hackle	Blue cock

CRAIG'S SLIDER

Hook	#8 L/S
Tail	Red wool
Body	Black Chenille
Rib	Flat silver tinsel
Wing	Black Pukeko or hen saddle
Hackle	Black cock
Head	Black deer hair clipped slider style

CRAIG'S LUMO

Definitely a night-time fly for mudeye hatches.

Hook	#8
Tail	Fluoro orange wool
Body	Fluoro wrap over white wool
Wing	Black Pukeko
Throat	Fluoro orange hackle
Head	Black thread varnished

CRUDDLER

Invented by "Diatribus", well known ACT angler Dalton Neville as a cross between a Craig's Night-time and a Muddler Minnow. It was first published in Freshwater Fishing Magazine #32 in Spring 1995.

Hook	#8
Butt	Red wool
Body	Green chenille
Wing	Black duck feather dyed green
Legs	Tips of deer hair from the head
Head Wrap	Deer hair
Head	Green chenille
Head cover	Pull down the butt end of deer from legs and tie off tightly
Note	This fly is tied with a distinct waist

CYCLOPS FLOATING YABBY

Well known commercial fly dresser, the late Murray 'MUZ" Wilson created this fly pattern. It is a bulky floating fly.

Note: Tie the foam back in first.

Hook	#6
Back	Round black foam split lengthways and will form the carapace and tail cover
Claws	2 bunches of rather bulky brown marabou and split by the carapace at the head
Body	Brown chenille
Rib	Copper wire
Body hackle	Soft brown cock

FUR FLY

Another Tony Sloane fly that has maximum movement and is most likely taken for a mudeye. Wet it well and fish it on a well-greased leader with a slow retrieve. The rabbit fur is taken from the lower back and cutting across the hide in 4mm strips. This is then cut into 15mm lengths for use as the body.

Hook	#8
Wing	15mm X 4mm strip of the winter hide of a rabbit Fold it in 4, wrap it around the shank and tie it in
Head	Black ostrich herl

FURY HAMILL'S KILLER

I first saw this fly being used by the late John 'Jed' Cunningham who used it extensively for lake fishing in Central Victoria. Varnish the head heavily with black nail polish.

Hook	#8-10
Tail	Black hackle fibres topped with Golden Pheasant tippets
Body	Green, yellow or red dubbing
Wing	Large bunch of green rabbit fur
Eyes	Small Jungle Cock. (Optional)

FUZZY WUZZY

This is another New Zealand fly invented in 1930 by Fred Fletcher. Originally tied in larger sizes to imitate freshwater crayfish, it has other good uses such as a caterpillar fly or smelt. For use as a caterpillar choose a smaller longer shank hook and dress it finer.

Hook	#6-8
Tail	Black squirrel
Body	Black, red, or green chenille or wool
Hackle	Long black hackles. On large flies up to three hackles may be needed and the fly tied in segments

FUZZY PURPLE

A bushy fly designed for night fishing. Lead wire is optional, but not for shallow lake margins at night.

Hook	#4-8
Tail	Black squirrel
Body	Purple wool
Hackle	Long black hen hackle tied thickly
Head	Well varnished black thread

GIANT WATER BEETLE

Rod Barford of "Fly Trek" supplied this pattern which imitates these beetles that are common in many freshwater lakes. Greenhill's Reservoir at Ararat in Victoria is one that comes to mind. The adult beetles are great fliers and migrate widely carrying eggs on the back of the male, making sure they are widespread.

Hook	#8 L/S
Body	Dark olive chenille with a band of white Antron tied underneath at the tail and pulled forward underneath the body to look like an air bubble
Legs	Peacock sword herls
Wing	Two brown hen or duck body feathers varnished black on the upper side
Head	Enlarged black thread heavily varnished

THE GENT

In other words, a maggot this is my tying for it

Hook	#10 SS O'Shannesy
Body	Off white wool
Back	3mm trip of clear plastic ribbed down with 3 kg nylon

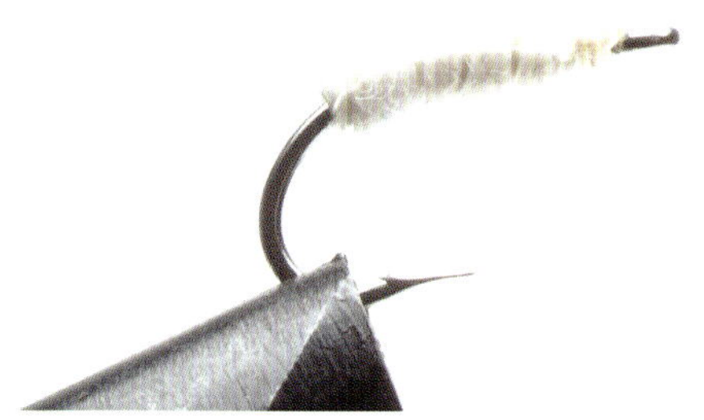

GREEN BEAST

An English fly known for fooling big fish by Alan Pearson.

Hook #8 L/S
Tail Green cock hackle fibres
Body Green floss tied carrot shape
Rib Fine silver wire
Hackle Brown partridge tied sparse

GREENHILL SPECIAL 

Probably a mudeye imitation for Greenhill Lake near Ararat, and invented by a member of the Ararat Fly Fishers Club.

Hook #6-10
Body Olive wool ribbed with gold wire
Wing Thick bunch of dyed green rabbit fur
Head Varnished well-formed tying thread

GREEN MACHINE 

This fly is from Canadian writer and angler Paul Marriner.

Hook #4-12 low water salmon
Tail Gold crystal flash
Tag Orange floss behind a tag of red wool
Body Spun green deer hair clipped to a cylinder
Hackle Green, palmered through the body

GREEN MEANY SHRIMP 

Origin unknown.

Hook #10
Tail Pale ginger hackle fibres
Underbody Fine lead wire
Legs Olive hen (sparse)
Body cover Heavy clear plastic strip
Body Pale olive seal fur teased out
Rib Clear plastic pot scrubber or similar

GREENWELL'S GLORY

A traditional English wet fly that has claimed a great many fish and is one of my 'go to' flies for river fishing. The brainchild of a certain Cannon Greenwell of Durham, (although others also make a claim to it) it is one of the most famous flies of them all. This is the pattern for the wet version, there is a separate listing in the dry fly section as it is well merited. I have fished this fly a lot in streams as an emergent caddis with good success. It is cast and retrieved straight across stream.

Hook	#12-14
Body	Waxed yellow silk
Rib	Fine gold wire sometimes used
Wing	Dark Starling or duck slips
Hackle	Light Cochybondu hen

GREY GHOST

A New Zealand 'Matuka' style smelt pattern that is ideal for Australian conditions.

Hook	#6-8
Body	Flat silver tinsel
Rib	Silver wire
Wing	Four white cock hackles dyed grey
Hackle	Grey cock

HAIRY DOG

Originally a Lake Taupo fly tied from black spaniel fur. In smaller sizes it is a good imitator of small hatching black midge, especially in the Snowy Mountains region. It is a great favourite of one of the better anglers I know, Mr. Norm King, who uses it extensively on midge hatches

Hook	#12 or even #14 L/S
Tail	Black spaniel or squirrel
Body	Black or red wool or fur dubbing tied sparsely
Rib	Silver tinsel
Wing	As for tail

HAMMILL'S KILLER

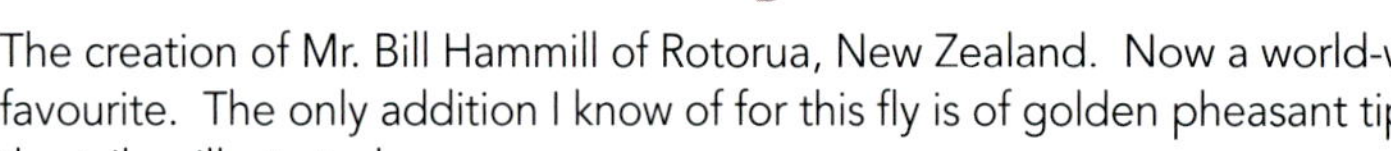

The creation of Mr. Bill Hammill of Rotorua, New Zealand. Now a world-wide favourite. The only addition I know of for this fly is of golden pheasant tippets to the tail as illustrated.

Hook	#4-10
Tail	Black squirrel tail with Golden Pheasant tippets on top
Body	Red, Yellow or green wool
Sides	Grey partridge feathers dyed green or golden olive
Eye	Red lurex diamond each side (optional)

HELLGRAMMITE 

Meant to imitate a toe biter or Dobson fly larvae. Note: Tie in the thorax palmer hackle before dubbing on the thorax

Hook	#10 L/S
Body	Dubbed hairs ear fur
Legs	Thin rubber
Thorax	As for body ribbed with the black hackle (see note)

HELTER SMELTER 

An original fly from Rick Keam, a retired fly dresser and writer, best known for his mudeye patterns that appear elsewhere in this book. This fly is very similar to another called the 'BMS' that appeared soon after this one. It was developed from Rick's 'Jiglet' series on a much longer hook with the addition of crystal flash at the suggestion of Peter Kirk.

Hook	#10-12 XXX/L
Tail	Sparse marabou broken off short
Body	Fine olive superfine dubbing well teased out for translucency
Rib	None
Flash	A single strand of pearl crystal flash on each side
Throat	Flat fluoro red thread, varnished
Head	Bright yellow glass bead

THE HENTY 

A sea trout fly from Tasmania, where there is a fair bit of this this type of fishing. I do not know the origin of this fly but it looks like a good whitebait imitation.

Hook	#10 L/S
Tail	Sparse white marabou
Body	Natural undyed seal fur teased out
Head	Red wool

HOT CAT 

By John Costello, a South African. South Africa has some excellent fly fishing and this is a favourite pattern from John's homeland. I have fished some of the areas there with excellent results.

Hook	#10-12
Tail	Medium ginger hackle reasonably thick
Body	Dubbed red seal fur palmered with soft ginger hackle
Rib	Silver oval tinsel
Head	Black thread

JB SPECIAL

From guide Jeff Brown of Emu Plains NSW. Jeff did not give a use for the fly though it is obviously a minnow/smelt pattern.

Hook	#1 X/L
Wing	2 or 3 white hackle feathers either side of the shank
Over-wing	White deer hair or goat fibres
Head	Packed white deer hair with a red deer hair band, trimmed slider style

KAKAHI QUEEN (WET)

A well-known New Zealand fly.

Hook	#10-12
Tail	Furnace hackle fibres
Body	Stripped peacock herl
Wing	Mallard or teal breast with a few stands dyed or marked yellow
Hackle	Furnace hen

KATE MCLAREN

The top dropper fly from Craig Coltman's team. Invented by Englishman Charles McLaren and named after his wife. This fly has caught lots of fish as a top dropper in lakes here in Australia and is regarded by many as an essential part of a team being fished. More often than not as a top dropper, it's a real favourite with a lot of very skilled competition anglers.

Hook	#10-12
Tail	Golden Pheasant topping or breast feather (not the barred tippets)
Body	Black seal fur tied thin
Rib	Oval fine silver tinsel
Hackle	Soft black cock, fully palmered

LIMITED EDITION 

Supplied by Ross Stewart, the only Australian to win a World Fly Fishing Championship. I have seen Ross catch a number of fish using this fly in Eildon Pondage. It was once restricted to members of the Northern Fly Fishers club, but I have since seen it referred to elsewhere. This fly is simple to tie and fishes well.

Hook	#8-10
Body	Red or green thin Mylar tubing or woven tinsel
Wing	Dark brown mink fur tied 'zonker' style
Rib	Fine gold or red wire

LIGHT GLOBE

An 'attractor' fly I first saw as a top dropper fly in Lake Wendouree when chasing year old rainbows. The theory being that the over bright fly would bring them in for a "what the devil is that look" and they would then take another fly in the team. It seemed to work but I can't remember who was using it. Old timer's disease?

Hook	#10 L/S
Body	Fluoro yellow or lime green wool
Wing	White marabou with two strands of herl from a peacock eye
Head	Well varnished black

MARABOU MUDDLER

A streamer fly based on the original Don Gapen Muddler Minnow design. This fly works well as a day or night. Mudeye fly in Victoria's western lakes.

Hook	#6-8
Tail	Red goose biots
Body	Gold braided tinsel
Wing	A bunch of olive marabou with 2 strands of Crystal Flash down each side
Head	Grey deer hair

MINK TADPOLE

This was a favoured pattern of Bill Classon for tadpole events in spring at Tarago Reservoir in Gippsland. Sadly frog numbers have seriously declined but this fly is a more than efficient mudeye pattern for evening and night mudeye hatches. Colours can also be varied, and olive would be useful.

Hook	#8
Tail	Black tanned mink skin cut to a 3mm strip
Body	Wound on strip of mink skin best cut on the cross
Note	The mink was furtively obtained from his mothers first stole

MRS. SIMPSON

A New Zealand pattern, originator unknown. There have been a number of quite different versions of this universally known fly and the one here is now the version accepted by most anglers. It is one of the world's most popular and killing flies. Story has is it that at the time of its invention Mrs. Wallis Simpson was extremely unpopular because of the abdication of the then King and this fly was named after her and intended to be a complete failure. How wrong can you be!

Hook	#4-8
Tail	Black squirrel tail
Body	Red or yellow wool
Side's	4 short cock pheasant green rump, 2 tied in at halfway, and 2 again at the head on both sides of hook

ORANGE AND OLIVE

A fly I have enjoyed great success with on Hepburn Lagoon, Victoria. It was likely taken for a small bug mudeye.

Hook	#8-10
Tail	Black hackle fibres
Butt	Fluoro orange chenille'
Body	Green chenille
Hackle	Brown partridge

PEDDER PARROT

Developed by two of the very best anglers I know and made especially for the huge fish that were caught in Lake Pedder in its best years. Norm King and S enator Shane Murphy created this successful and colourful edition to our angling history.

Hook	#8
Body	Dubbed orange seal fur, teased out
Rib	Fine gold wire
Wing	Dark black cat strip matuka style. Mink at a pinch-pinch (Feral cat recommended)
Overwing	Peacock sword herl
Head	Fine black dubbing

PENNELL AND BLACK

Another loch style favourite of mine. Often fished on the point in a team of unweighted flies. I have taken many fish on it.

Hook	#10-12
Tail	Golden Pheasant tippets
Rib	Fine oval silver tinsel
Body	Tip of oval tinsel then black floss
Hackle	Three turns soft black cock

POACHER

Another quite common name for a fly, I believe it to be of Scottish origin. I found it in the John Veniard book "Fly Dressers' Guide" and made a variant I thought would work. I have caught lots of fish on it, mostly as a middle dropper of wet flies when fishing from boats. Most effective during dun hatches when the fish aren't yet up. I have given it to lots of my friends who have also had good success with it. Craig Coltman from Ballarat wrote of it *"Dear Rob. I once met an old prick who gave me a wonderful fly he called the Poacher. It has proven to be a realistic middle dropper in a team of nymphs. I have used it with great success both in Victoria and Tasmania and it won a session for me lake fishing in the world championships in Scotland, thanks Rob"*.
Note: I use thin fluoro orange wool for the first third of the body. How or why I substituted it for the original tying I have no idea. I do know it is my most successful innovation, but more than likely not original.

Hook	#12
Tail	Red fibres from Golden Pheasant body feather
Body	First third orange floss or dubbed seal fur, remainder bronze peacock herl
Hackle	Red/brown hen

RAINBOW KILLER

I have used this fly with some success fished straight across large rivers on a sinking line.

Hook	#10
Underbody	Lead wire
Tail	Red wool
Butt	Silver oval tinsel
Thorax	Peacock herl
Hackle	Black hen

RED ARSED BASTARD

I have used this fly for many years. It may be a New Zealand pattern, but I am unsure of this. This is the wet pattern used as a beetle or a snail and fished ultra-slow. For some reason it works well on brown trout, they seem to be rather partial to red. There is also a longtail and dry fly version.

Hook	#10-16
Tail	Red floss
Body	Rear half red floss
Thorax	Peacock herl
Hackle	Black hen tied sparse

RED SPOT SHRIMP

The red spot is tied in first and trimmed after the fly has been formed

Hook	#8 caddis bend
Underbody	Fine lead wire
Back	4mm strip clear heavy plastic
Body	Pale olive seal fur well teased out
Red Spot	Thick red wool
Rib	3kg mono

RICK'S MINNOW

From Rick Massie who fishes it to smelting trout

Hook	#10 L/S
Tail	Dyed green mallard
Body	Flat holographic tinsel
Back	As for tail
Rib	Narrow holographic tinsel or just wire
Throat	Red seals fur clipped short
Eyes	Small stick on
Body	On completion coat the whole body with Loon Soft Head

RON PENNEY'S WET FLY

Ron is also well known as the originator of the Penney knot. This is the most reliable leader to fly knot I know. It is quick to tie and can be found on the internet.
A favourite of Ron Penny who worked at the Compleat Angler store in Melbourne.

Hook	#8
Tail	Thick olive wool
Body	Alternate bands of brown and olive Chenille
Wing	Olive marabou with grey pukeko or substitute over the top to hold the marabou in place
Throat	Dyed olive partridge

ROSELLA

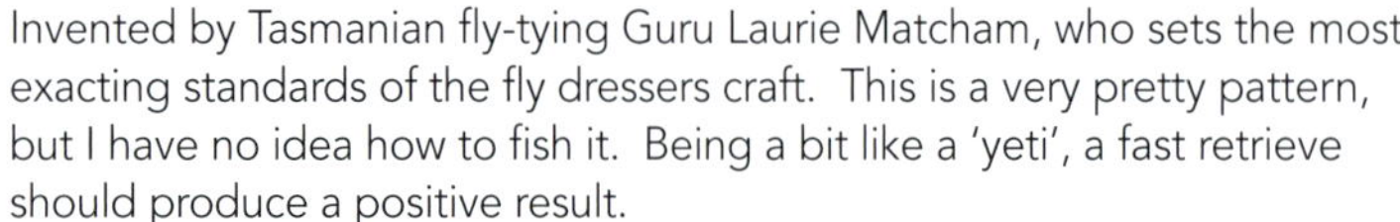

Invented by Tasmanian fly-tying Guru Laurie Matcham, who sets the most exacting standards of the fly dressers craft. This is a very pretty pattern, but I have no idea how to fish it. Being a bit like a 'yeti', a fast retrieve should produce a positive result.

Hook	#8
Tail	Golden Pheasant tippets
Body	Rear half dubbed yellow mohair, front half red mohair
Wing	Black mink strip
Overwing	Peacock herl
Eyes	Jungle cock

SCHOOLGIRL SMELT

There are lots of smelt patterns around and this is another that woks. Fish it fast.

Hook	#6-10
Tail	Nil
Body	Fluoro white wool or dubbing
Wing	Sparse white rabbit to extend to 6mm beyond the round of the hook
Head	Well-formed white varnished thread
Eyes	Black varnish spots or silver stick-on eyes

SMELT JONES

Vastly experienced angler, author and guide, Philip Weigall fishes with this pattern.

His drawing of the fly is very basic and he wrote: "you can see why I gave up a career as an artist and took up fishing". *"This is a fly I use, but it's not necessarily better than several others. I suspect the fly is less important than its presentation, and the erratic behaviour of smelting trout. Give it a try anyway"*

Hook	#6-10 L/S
Tail	White green mix of hair
Body	Dubbed dull green seal fur overlaid with milky plastic so you can just make out the greenish tinge
Wing	A single tuft of wallaby hair, 'Tom Jones' style
Eye	Silver stick-on eyes or sequin with painted pupil

STONKER

The wing on this fly tends to wrap around the body, so I prefer to rib it down 'matuka' style.

Hook #6-10
Body Dubbed red seals fur
Rib Silver oval tinsel
Wing Thin grey rabbit 'zonker' strip tied in at the head only, or ribbed down with tinsel
Overwing Barred teal or wood duck fibres
Throat Orange hackle fibres

SHRIMP

From late Bruce Smith.

Hook #10-12 caddis bend
Underbody Bunch of teal breast feathers also form the legs
Body Clear Tiewell Midge Lace
Eyes Medium black mono (burnt)
Antennae Two moose mane fibres

ROB'S SHRIMP

One of my own?

Hook #8-10 wide gape
Tail Pale olive hackle fibres
Carapace 5mm wide strip of fairly thick plastic bag
Body Pale olive dubbing
Rib Gold wire
Thorax Pale olive dubbing
Hackle 3 turns of soft grizzle
Feelers Two moose mane fibres

BARLEY SHRIMP

Rod Barford gives his version of this common freshwater crustacean.

He teases out the fur under the thorax for legs.

Hook #8-10 Tiemco 400T
Body Blended seal fur, 80% natural, 10% yellow and 10% olive
Carapace Clear plastic back covering cut to shape with a plastic tag extended over the bend for a tail
Rib Fine gold wire to the abdomen only
Eyes Burnt nylon

CANADIAN SHRIMP

This was one of the first flies in my collection in the 1970's and came from a Canadian, Prof. Ian Weeks.

Hook	# 2-6 Low water salmon
Butt	Gold oval tinsel
Feelers	Squirrel tail
Hackle	Grizzle
Eye	Nylon
Body	Yellow floss
Carapace	Clear plastic or acetate from a chocolate box
Rib	Black thread

SNAIL

Arthur Frith. Snails form a large part of the food chain at certain times of the year. This is a pattern that imitates them well. It is a very simple fly. Try winding the herl and the thread together to make a more robust body. Fish it static or with an ultra-slow figure 8 retrieve.

Hook	#12-14
Hook	#14-18
Thread	Black
Tag	White floss tied in at the head
Body	One strand of peacock herl

SNAIL

A variant on the standard snail adapted by Peter Coulson.

Hook	#10-14 mostly 12
Body	Peacock herl
Hackle	Small duck breast feather swept back

FLOATING SNAIL

When snails are prolific mostly in spring it is common to see trout just bulging when they take them. Aquatic snails often crawl on the underside of the surface film feeding on minute algae and are easily picked off by trout. A parachute hackled fly sits just where it needs to be. A floating snail left to dead drift near a moving fish will often get the desired response. Wait till the line tightens before lifting.

Hook	#14
Body	Peacock Herl
Post	White Hi-Vis
Hackle	Black cock

SOLDIER PALMER COACHMAN

Another Czech fly from Dr. Holas Vladimir, whom I met in 1996.

Hook	#8-10
Tail	Golden Pheasant tippet
Body	Peacock herl
Palmer	Soft brown cock hackle
Rib	Fine silver oval tinsel
Wing	White duck slips or white hair wing
Throat	Dark brown hackle

SPIDER

Hook	#14-16
Body	Dark brown thread
Thorax	Brown seal fur
Hackle	One turn brown hen a little larger than normal

SUNSET FLY

Originated by Tasmanian Tony Sloane. This fly works well in failing light. The original pattern calls for a floss body, but I prefer and tie my own with very slim dubbed seal fur.

Hook	#6-10
Tail	Black hackle
Body	Yellow floss
Hackle	From the back forward, 40% yellow, 20% red and 40% black
Head	Well-formed black varnish

TADPOLE

Noel Jetson. This fly was a favourite for the early season Tasmanian tadpole events, especially in Lake Sorrell. Regrettably the frog population has drastically declined.

Hook	#12
Tail	Black hen hackle fibres in a bunch
Body	Mixed black and red seal fur
Hackle	Longish soft black cock

TRANSFORMER

A successful nighttime fly supplied by Mr. Aussie Angler himself, Rick Dobson. Predominately used in New Zealand, it also works here. Rick suggests fishing it with a slow but constant figure 8 retrieve.

Hook	#6-8 heavy wire.
Tail	Orange 'glo-bug' yarn tied in at the head and bound down all of the hook shank
	It is tied this way to avoid making bulges in the body
Body	Pale greenish 'lumo' in 2 sections
Wings (2)	Clumps of purple marabou at halfway point and at the head. Tied 'Tom Jones' style
	Add a few strands of UV flash in each clump
Head	Orange flat waxed thread

UBL (UGLY BLACK LEECH)

This pattern was given to me by a French journalist, "Affre Piere", who says 'make it any colour you like as long as it is black' and it is 'good for anything that swims'.

Hook	#4-8
Tail	Black rabbit 'zonker' strip
Body	Wound on 'zonker' strip cut on angle

WATSONS FANCY

Another of those English wets with a yellow tail that ideally suits Australian conditions. The red and yellow combination works. Try it as a top dropper fly in lakes.

Hook	#10-12
Tail	Golden Pheasant toppings with the natural curve upward
Body	Halved, rear red seal fur, front black
Rib	Silver oval tinsel
Wing	Crow
Hackle	Black hen

WICKHAMS FANCY

An English fly of the 1880's that two Mr. Wickhams claimed as their originals. G.E.M. Skues gives credit to Dr. T.C Wickham for inventing it. I have caught lots of trout retrieving it slowly in the surface film as it fishes well as an emerging caddis imitation. A wingless variety is good also.

Hook	#12
Tail	Guinea fowl fibres dyed red/brown or simple ginger hackle fibres
Body	Flat gold tinsel
Rib	Fine gold wire
Body	Palmer ginger hackle tied in at the back and wound forward
Wing	Pale to medium wild duck wing slips
Hackle	Ginger cock
Hackle	Black hen

WILLOW GRUB

The grubs are larvae of a saw fly wasp, 'Nematus oligospilus', which is endemic to the northern hemisphere. They turned up in New Zealand in the 1990's and were first noticed in mainland Australia around 2005. The grubs are about 2cm long and the pale green adults 6-8 mm and similar in appearance to adult caddis. The grubs can appear in early November and are usually finished by late February. Trout become completely engrossed with them as they are easy prey and there are plenty of them. Grubs can completely strip a willow tree. Trout simply sit under a willow and mop them up as they fall in.
Colours vary from lime green to a straw colour and everywhere in-between, but lime green flies fish best. The adults will catch fish also, but the grubs are much easier to fish and tie. The fly is very simple to make from those lime green wormy looking soft balls with flashing lights that kids throw around and available in $2 shops. A more often used alternative is 2mm lime green foam sheet cut into 2mm wide strips. This foreign invader was thought to be the answer to reducing willow tree invasion. However, it seems to be in decline due to the ever-expanding numbers of European wasps that feed greedily on the grubs.

Hook	#14
Thread	Lime green
Body	Lime green foam or plastic

WORM

I got this fly from a Tasmanian friend at an Australian Championship event at Falls Creek in Victoria, and it was recommended as a fly to use after rain. Rain was forecast, lo and behold overnight we got about 75mm and by next morning water levels were rising. My first beat was on the Bundara River with the water colouring and slowly rising. Wondering what to fish with I remembered the worm fly and tied it on. Three nice fish and two more lost was a good result and won me the session. The afternoon session was on the Upper Mitta Mitta River near the Blue Duck. The river was up about 600mm, dirty and rising rapidly, so I tried the worm again. The fishing was very difficult to say the least, but I still managed one and lost another. Since then I haven't seen the same conditions, but I look forward to the next time. It is good to know what to try in coloured water with a fair chance of success.

Hook	#8 XXXXL shank
Underbody	Lead wire and
Body	Bright pink wool
Overbody	A wrapped strip of latex from a c ondom about 4mm wide
Rib	2-3 Kg monofilament

YELLOW TAILED STICK FLY

Provided by Craig Coltman. This fly is part of a regular team he fishes on Lake Wendouree.

Hook	#12-14
Tail	Golden pheasant toppings
Body	Single layer of peacock herl
Hackle	Brown
Head	Fluoro yellow thread

YABBY

My first experience with this fly was on a trip to Lake Toolondo in Victoria in oily calm conditions. Explaining to my client to look for a rocking of the reflection from the water surface to indicate a moving fish, and soon after there was a movement visible at extreme casting distance. The person with me was totally incapable of casting that distance unfortunately, so I took the rod and waded out to the top of my waders, and in doing so I just managed to reach the area where I had seen the bulge. A short sink time and slow figure 8 saw the line tighten and a heavy drag on the line. On landing it turned out to be a large turtle. After playing hide and seek with its head for a time as I was trying to get the hook out, it was finally unhooked and released. A few minutes later at the same range another bulge and yet another turtle. I have never caught one since that happened in about 1990 and have never heard of another.

Hook	#6-8 heavy wire.
Tail	Orange 'glo-bug' yarn tied in at the head and bound down all of the hook shank. It is tied this way to avoid making bulges in the body
Body	Pale greenish 'lumo' in 2 sections
Wings (2)	Clumps of purple marabou at halfway point and at the head. Tied 'Tom Jones' style Add a few strands of UV flash in each clump
Head	Orange flat waxed thread.

YETI

Max Christensen. An evergreen successful and favourite fly. I have tied hundreds of these for various clients and they always come back for more.

Hook	#8
Tail	Orange cock hackle fibres
Rib	Gold wire
Body	Black marabou silk
Wing	A strip of dyed black seal fur on the skin or black musquash
Hackle	Black
Eyes	Red Lurex diamonds set into each side of the black varnished head

---

ZULU

Another of my favourites for loch style fishing.

Hook	#12
Tail	Red wool
Body	Loosely dubbed black seal fur, teased out
Rib	Fine flat silver tinsel
Hackle	Black cock

WOOLLY BUGGERS

No serious fly box would be complete without these proven fish takers. They are of American origin and one Russell Blessing is credited with developing the pattern. Woolly Buggers come in a wide variety of sizes and a whole spectrum of colours. Originally, they were made large for big fish and they work as imitations of bait fish, damsels, leeches and other aquatic animals. I also like them in smaller sizes as damsel fly nymphs, dragon fly larvae and even caddis larvae in much smaller sizes. Some of the other patterns in this book are variants of this basic fly. For my personal use I like to tie in a fluorescent butt on the body, using red, yellow, orange or chartreuse. The tail can vary from thick to thin in various lengths. It can also be highlighted with the addition of flashy or fluorescent tinsels to the tail. The addition of a bead of brass, copper or coloured tungsten and/or lead wire under the body changes the fishing capabilities greatly. I have illustrated a couple of my favourites. Note: the addition of a 1cm piece of 3kg mono before tying in the tail is a must to prevent the annoyance of the marabou tail getting wrapped around the bend of the hook.

WOOLLY BUGGER

Hook #4-14
Tail A bunch of marabou feather. (colour of choice)
Rib Tinsel to suit
Body Chenille. (colour of choice)
Palmer Hackle to suit. (colour of choice)
Note All black is the basic fly

FLUORO WOOLLY BUGGER

A John Rumpf recommendation for failing light and darkness.

Hook #6-8
Tail Black marabou with fluoro tinsel
Body Fluorescent wrap. (colour of choice)
Hackle Large black cock palmered with extra at the head

DIRTY HARRY

Stuart Rees. These are Stuart's variations for Australian conditions of flies derived from flies by the former world champion angler Hywell Morgan whose fly was called 'humungous'. Hywell is the son of the equally famous Welshman Moc Morgan. Hywell proved the effectiveness of the pattern on the Eildon Pondage some years ago on a captain's tour of Australia. I had the privilege of fishing with him at a national championship in Tasmania in the 1990's. He was a former world casting champion and his skills were amazing. At the time he was using 3 heavily weighted flies on a 6m cast and after 3 hours casting more than a whole fly line, there was not a wind knot to be found. If only I could cast like that!

Hook #6-8
Tail Longish marabou
Flash Flat fine Lurex
Body Crystal chenille
Body hackle Black or to match chosen colour
Head Tungsten bead

CZECH BUGGER

From Dr. Holas Vladimir at the Czesky Krumlov World Championships in 1996. This fly is an interesting variant on the woolly bugger.

Hook	#6 L/S
Tail	Olive marabou 4cm long with pearl Flashabou about 15mm long
Rib	Silver tinsel
Body	Peacock herl
Hackle	Large red cock
Head	3mm brass bead

BUGGER ME

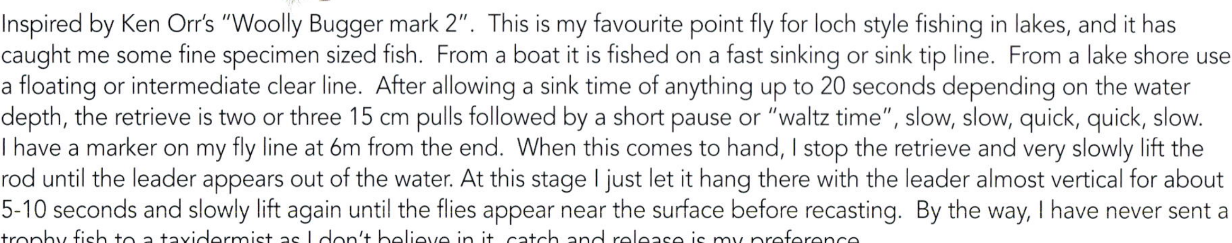

Inspired by Ken Orr's "Woolly Bugger mark 2". This is my favourite point fly for loch style fishing in lakes, and it has caught me some fine specimen sized fish. From a boat it is fished on a fast sinking or sink tip line. From a lake shore use a floating or intermediate clear line. After allowing a sink time of anything up to 20 seconds depending on the water depth, the retrieve is two or three 15 cm pulls followed by a short pause or "waltz time", slow, slow, quick, quick, slow. I have a marker on my fly line at 6m from the end. When this comes to hand, I stop the retrieve and very slowly lift the rod until the leader appears out of the water. At this stage I just let it hang there with the leader almost vertical for about 5-10 seconds and slowly lift again until the flies appear near the surface before recasting. By the way, I have never sent a trophy fish to a taxidermist as I don't believe in it, catch and release is my preference.

Hook	#8
Underbody	Lead wire
Tail	Black marabou with four strands of pearl flashabou
Butt	Fluoro orange chenille
Body	Black chenille
Rib	Gold wire
Hackle	Black softish cock fully palmered but not over the butt

MARK 2 WOOLLY BUGGER

Adapted by Ken Orr, which soon became a standard.

Hook	#8-10
Tail	Black marabou with side flashes of orange marabou
Body	Olive Chenille
Rib	Silver tinsel is optional
Hackle	Palmered soft black cock

SHREK

I first saw this fly during an Australian fly fishing championship on Little Pine Lagoon in Tasmania. If you didn't have one during that time, you almost certainly went fishless. Tasmanian and Australian representative Joe Riley came up with the pattern that is proving to be one of the best Tassie patterns ever. Well done Joe.

Hook	#10/L/S
Thread	Fluoro orange
Tail	Olive marabou with Blue and olive crystal flash. 1 ½ - 2 hook shank lengths
Body	Green holographic tinsel
Rib	Red wire
Palmer	Black hackle
Head	Tungsten or glass bead

BLACK THING

Hook #6 XXL
Tail 10 strands pearl Crystal Flash either side of a pair of grizzle hackle feathers
Body Gold, green or red plaited tinsel string
Wing Black and red marabou with red crystal flash on the outside
Collar Black cross-cut rabbit wound on
Head Red brass bead
Weed guard 10kg mono is optional

BOMBER BOY

This is a deer hair popper and floats well, but it will need dry fly floatant if fished for an extended time.

Hook #6
Tail Two dyed red hen saddle feathers curved outward.
Body Compressed bands of red and black deer hair with a roundish profile from the top
Eyes 7cm stick on doll eyes

CHERNOBYL ANT

Hook #4-6 XL
Body 4mm Black closed cell foam over black thread and cemented in place.
Wing Black deer hair with crystal flash sides
Thorax Black wool
Head Cover 2mm black foam strip
Marker 2mm yellow foam

CLARRIE HALL MUDEYE

I have had some fantastic success with this simple fly, catching Australian bass in Clarrie Hall Dam in the Tweed Valley. It was most effective in the early summer when there are lots of cicadas in the air and plenty of mudeyes in the water. Bass are very aggressive, ambush predators and absolutely smash a surface fly. Basically, a mudeye with a muddler head, it is well greased and used like a popper or allowed to sink a bit if not treated with floatant. From a drifting boat it was cast in amongst the dead trees or gaps in the water lilies and pulled out with a smart jerky retrieve. No worries about takes, but much more difficulty in stopping a fish from snagging. Colours can be varied to suit.

Hook #8 wet fly
Tail Olive goose biots split and tied short
Body Olive chenille
Wing One brown partridge feather 2/3 body length and tied flat
Head Compacted deer hair with some left as legs after trimming

CORK POPPER

Tie and cement on the tapered headfirst, then apply the paint. These flies are easier to make in batches and can be in a variety of colours. The body should be grooved on the underside and glued in position.

Hook	Suitable size for the cork which is halved length ways and shaped
Underbody	Black thread
Tail	Black cock hackles splayed
Hackle	Large dyed black cock
Eyes	Painted or stick on

FOAM BEETLE

Work it like a popper. After casting, allow it to sit before popping, and repeat the process. Takes will be hard and explosive.

Hook	#6-10L/S
Back	Black foam
Body	Peacock herl
Palmer	Black cock hackle
Thorax	Peacock herl
Legs	Black rubber
Head	Black rubber

FREDDO FROG

Named in honour of my late dad.

Hook	#4-6
Legs	Green deer hair or rubber with black or dark green knuckles
Body	Compacted deer hair, light brown or fawn under a green top
Eyes	Black 7mm stick on doll eyes

FURRY HAMILLS KILLER

Another mudeye style fly, but bigger.

Hook	#6-8
Tail	Thick black cock hackle with a few stands of Golden Pheasant tippet on top
Body	Dyed green rabbit
Wings	Dyed green rabbit bunches at halfway point and at the head
Head	Black varnished thread

FUZZY WUZZY

Hook	#6-10
Tail	Black hackle fibres
Body	Halved, rear bright purple wool front black chenille
Hackle	Centre large claret, front large black cock. All tied heavily
Head	Varnished black thread

GAMBUSIA

An introduced species that has now become a common forage fish.

Hook	#8-10
Tail	Very pale green SLF or similar
Body	Ice chenille coloured with a light green marking pen
Eyes	Small black and silver stick-ons

MOUSE

Uses lots of deer hair but attracts slashing strikes. Allow it to sit a few seconds before a very fast rolly-polly, stop start, or slow but steady or retrieve.

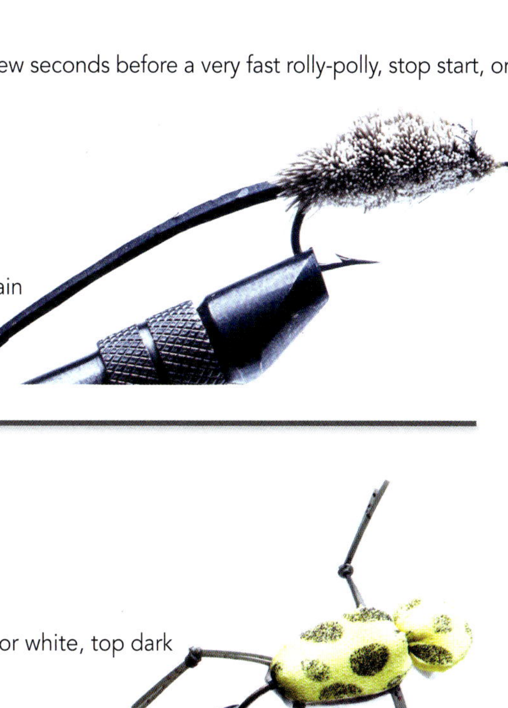

Hook	#6 L/S
Tail	10cm strip of black leather
Body	Compressed deer hair
Whiskers	Leave a few strands from the collar
Eyes	Spots of black varnish or black plastic bead chain
Weed guard	optional

RUBBER FROG

Foam sheet is available in a spotted format in various colours.

Hook	#6-8 L/S
Body	2 mm foam in two halves. Bottom light brown or white, top dark green and spotted yellow
Legs	Green rubber

RUBBER FROG

Foam sheet is available in a spotted format in various colours.

Hook	#6-8 L/S
Body	2 mm foam in two halves. Bottom light brown or white, top dark green and spotted yellow
Legs	Green rubber

TIGER POPPER

Hook	#6-8
Tails	One pair each of black and yellow hen saddle feathers
Body	Compressed bands of yellow and black deer hair with a roundish profile from the top
Eyes	Stick on doll eyes

WOOLLY BUGGER

Yes, them again, because THEY WORK! Red and black, green, or brown are all good colours.

Hook	#6-8
Tail	Black marabou with crystal flash
Butt	Fluoro orange chenille.
Rib	Silver tinsel.
Body	Black chenille.
Hackle	Large black cock hackle

YELLOW MONDAY

This is one of a number of names for the common large green cicada that is widespread in Australia.

Hook	#6 XL/s
Body	Clipped compressed green deer hair with an oval profile from above
Wings	Broad hen grizzle feather tied flat
Head	Clipped deer hair trimmed diamond shaped
Eyes	Red glass beads on mono

MURRAY COD

My memories of Murray Cod go back to the late 1940's when as a young boy I saw cod being caught on bait, and on 'Aeroplane' spinners. The interesting thing about the latter was the use by the then old timers of yellow and/or red feathers tied to the treble hooks at the rear end of what were very large lures with blades up to 20cm across. The preferred yellow feathers were from the crest of Sulphur Crested Cockatoos, (now totally protected), but they considered that colour as the most important. In a moment of experimentation at a Melbourne Boat Show many years ago the native fish association had a cod in a large glass tank. I tried all sorts of colours at the end of the tank to see if there was any reaction. Eventually yellow was tried and the cod flared its gills and charged the opposite end of the tank hitting the end with much force. No other colour had any reaction at all. Other colours that seem to work sometimes are all black, red and black, yellow, green or chartreuse. I have also taken a small cod on a pink and yellow cod fly. These flies can be made with large marabou feathers or rabbit zonker strips or a combination of both.
Try any of these flies on Barramundi as well!

YELLOW AND RED COD FLY

This pattern is adapted from the flies used on big salmonids in Alaska.

Hook	#2/0-4 low water salmon or similar
Tail	Bright yellow marabou with pearl crystal flash
Body	Rear half, wrapped yellow rabbit zonker cut on the cross with a few stands of crystal flash at the front Front half, the same in red rabbit
Eyes	Gold dumbbell

BLACK AND PURPLE COD FLY

Hook	#2/0 LWS
Tail	Purple marabou with purple crystal flash
Body	Rear 1/2 shocking pink rabbit crosscut zonker, Front ½ black
Head	Silver dumbbell head

CHARTREUSE AND GREEN COD FLY

Hook	2/0 LWS
Tail	Green marabou with pearl crystal flash
Body	In thirds, 1st wrapped green rabbit zonker strip, then chartreuse, then green
Eyes	Gold dumbbell

BLACK AND RED COD FLY

Hook	#2/0 LWS
Tail	Thick bunch of black Marabou with crystal flash
Body	Rear third, red rabbit zonker strip, middle black rabbit, front red
Eyes	Black dumbbell

SALTWATER FLIES

BASS YABBY

After the feelers and eyes, the thorax is tied and covered with the plastic after which the tail body is made. Some of my later versions of this fly have an orange chenille thorax.

Hook	#10 XLS stainless
Underbody	Lead wire
Feelers	Polar bear mixed with long white cock hackle
Eyes	Burnt nylon
Claws	Large white hen feathers cut to shape
Carapace	A strip of thick clear plastic bag also to cover the tail
Thorax	White wool palmered with white hackle
Tail	White hen saddle clipped short over white wool
Rib	Silver tinsel wrap
Tail	Plastic wrap trimmed to shape

BLACK AND PINK

Weed guards of 12kg mono for snaggy water.

Hook	#3/0 SS
Wing	Three pairs of black cock saddle feathers, overlaid on each side by a dark grizzle saddle feather and pink and pearl Flashabou
Collar	Pink rabbit fur
Head	Black chenille
Eyes	Black and silver stick-ons
Head	Epoxy

BAITED BREATH

Colours of this fly can be varied, pale green and white are also recommended.

Hook	#2 SS
Legs	White Marabou with crystal flash
Body	White chenille palmered with white hackle
Eyes	Pearl plastic with painted on eyes

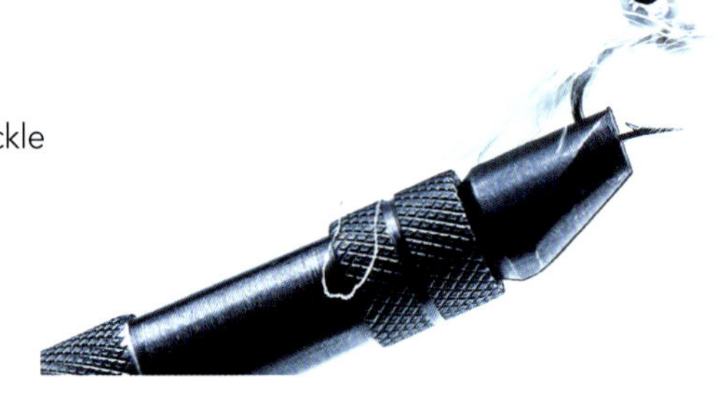

CUBE FLY

Mike Winterton designed this fly to look like a pilchard head. He uses it as a general saltwater fly in a pilchard berley trail. Made for Yellowfin and Albacore tuna, it will also take other tuna species plus snapper, kingfish, barracouta, mackerel and shark.

Hook Tarpon #7/0
Tail Red/brown marabou
Body Compacted white deer hair
Thorax Red marabou
Head Blue deer hair
Eyes Large silver stick-ons

DAHLBERG DIVER

A barramundi or bass fly by Robert John with the pseudonym "Cochybondhu", whose advice is to fish it slowly. This fly has no body as such, just a wing and compacted deer hair head. A weed guard of 10kg mono is an option for weedy or snaggy locations. Many different colours can be used according to location and light conditions.

Hook #2-6
Tail Long hackle feathers and pearl crystal flash
Head Compacted layers of deer hair trimmed to shape
Weed Guard Optional

FLATHEAD BENDBACK

This fly is from Steve Starling, best known for his TV and DVD appearances, and also the promotion of certain soft plastic lures. Bead chain eyes may be added to the fly, this will decrease snag and weed resistance as it will cause the fly to run upside down.

Hook #3L/S bent to ride upside down
Tail Short red wool or Fishair
Underbody Metallic blue tinsel over lead wire
Overbody Silver Mylar tubing
Wing In three layers, white Bucktail then a few stands of Crystal Flash with sparse chartreuse bucktail on top
Head Well formed with painted eyes or small stick-ons

FUSILIER

Hook 4/0 SS O'Shannesy
Tail Trimmed yellow cock saddle hackles cemented into silver Mylar tube
Body Wrapped silver Mylar
Underwing Four blue dyed saddle hackles. Two each side
Overwing Three parts, top silver Flashabou, over green and chartreuse
Throat Blue Flashabou
Eyes Gold dumbbell with pupil

GOLD BOMBER

A renowned barramundi fly. Weed guards of 12kg mono for snaggy water.

Hook	#3/0-2 SS
Thread	White
Rattle	20mm plastic rattle tied in underneath and well glued down
Wing	Gold holographic sparkle-flash
Eyes	7mm stick-ons

BLACK AND GRIZZLE

This is an original Lefty Kreh fly.

Hook	2/0 SS O'Shannesy
Tail	Black hackle with grizzle at the sides
Thorax	Black hackle
Eyes	Bead chain

HAYNSEY'S RATTLIN SHRIMP

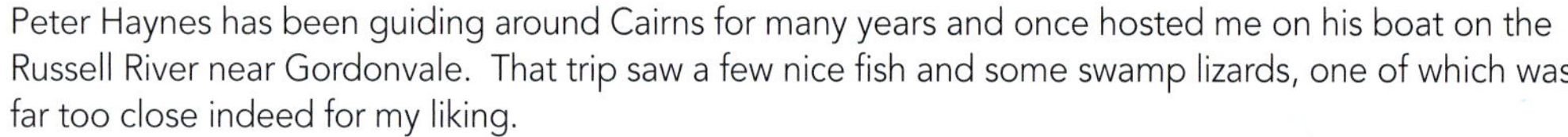

Peter Haynes has been guiding around Cairns for many years and once hosted me on his boat on the Russell River near Gordonvale. That trip saw a few nice fish and some swamp lizards, one of which was far too close indeed for my liking.

Hook	#1/0-2 SS
Feelers	6 strands of white Fishair.
Body	Small plastic rattle covered with Mylar tubing
Hackle	Long white cock
Eyes	Stick-on 3mm black and silver
Method	1. Bind the rattle onto the hook shank and cement in place 2. Tie in the 'feelers' to extend 3cm beyond the bend of the hook 3. Wind on 3 turns of white hackle behind the rattle and whip finish 4. Slide the Mylar over the eye of the hook and tie down the hook eye end only 5. Stick on the eyes one each side and cover with 5 min epoxy

SINCLAIR'S SCUDDER

A fly from Roger Sinclair to fish at Corroboree Billabong for Barramundi and Saratoga.

Hook	4/0 SS O'Shannesy
Weed guard	20kg mono.
Tail	Red Hackle feathers with black Bucktail and pearl crystal flash overlaid with red marabou
Head	Foam covered in electrical heat shrink wrap
Note:-	Tie in the foam under the head at each end and glue it down. The shrink is the laid over the top and carefully heated to shrink it to shape. This will take some practice

MUD THING

Supplied by Scott Mitchell, originally of Alpine Angler store fame. This is a barramundi fly for use in dirty water. Add weed guards of 12kg mono for snaggy water

Hook	#4/0-1/0. With nylon weed guard
Wing	Bucktail over dyed yellow grizzle saddle feathers with gold Flashabou
Eyes	Bead chain or dumbbells depending on water flow and depth
Collar	Black Zonker strip wound on

PILCHARD HEAD

A Peter Coulson fly. Specially designed for berley trail use. Allow plenty of sink time before a fast retrieve.

Hook	#3/0-1 SS
Butt	Large clump of red and black Slinky fibre. Tied in above the barb and trimmed off at the bend
Wing	White Slinky fibre overwrapped with silver Sparkle-Flash
Overwing	Grey Slinky fibre
Eyes	7mm yellow stick-ons
Finish	Marked in suitable colour with waterproof markers Coat with three coats of "Softdip"

PINK THING

A fly designed for barramundi and other saltwater species by Graham White of Darwin. The pattern was provided by well-known publisher and fishing identity Alex Julius. Add weed guards of 12kg mono for snaggy water.

Hook	2/0 SS Mustad 34007
Wing	White saddle hackles with a grizzle overlay on each side
Tinsel	Pearl Crystal Flash may be added to the wing
Collar	Dyed fluoro pink rabbit fur
Eyes	2 beads of 3mm bead chain

PETERS PINK THING

On a recent trip to Cairns with my son Peter I caught in excess of 25 Barra on this fly. Add weed guards of 12kg mono for snaggy water.

Hook	#2/0 SS O'Shannesy.
Wing	Light purple Flashabou over white Flashabou
Collar	Fluoro pink rabbit
Eyes	Gold or silver dumbbell with pupils

PUPPY DOG SMELT

Provided by Peter Coulson who for some years tied a superb range of saltwater flies under the title "Dog Tooth". Peter has since retired from tying, but his patterns are published in his book, "Australian Fly Patterns", which is now out of print. Note: A small amount of epoxy is needed to hold the wing slightly flat and keep the eye from coming off. This also applies to other flies with Stick-on eyes. Add weed guards of 12kg mono for snaggy water if desired.

Hook	#1/0-4 Stainless
Body	Nil.
Wing	Sparkle-Flash Belly Shine with a pearl lateral line
Eyes	7mm 3D stick-ons
Head	White thread

ROB'S SHRIMP

Hook	#12 L/S stainless bent to look like a caddis bend
Tail	Pale olive hackle fibres.
Carapace	5mm wide strip of fairly thick plastic bag
Eyes	Burnt mono
Body	Pale olive dubbing
Rib	Gold wire
Thorax	Pale olive dubbing
Hackle	3 turns of soft grizzle

SALTWATER SHRIMP

Courtesy of Dee Wallace, the skipper of mothership French Look 2.

I obtained this during the first Black Marlin Fly Fishing Championship in Cairns in 1996.

The owner John Paul Richards was obsessed with catching a marlin on a fly with ultra-light backing (6lb?) to his fly line. To my knowledge he is unsuccessful.

Hook	#1-2 X/L shank
Eyes	Bead chain
Feelers	Two splayed Grizzle hackle feathers
Body	Pearl Mylar palmered with badger or grizzle hackle to the thorax
Back	2 or 3 dark grizzle hackles ribbed down with fine wire
Tail	Clipped feathers extended from the back

SHEPPARD'S DELIGHT

I tied this pattern for well-known coarse angler and sometime fly fisher Terry Sheppard.

Hook	2/0 Stainless
Tail	2 white saddle hackles back to back with well-marked grizzle on the outside
Body	Flat silver tinsel ribbed with silver wire
Wing	Chartreuse Fishair, with pearl Crystal Flash, then blue Fishair with thin green Lurex on top
Throat	Orange wool
Head	Black thread with a chartreuse band, painted eyes and clear varnished

SONIC SQUID

A favourite saltwater fly from Adelaide fly fisher Dave Bennett.

Hook #6 SS Long shank
Tentacles White Marabou and silver crystal flash
Wing Thick latex rubber
Body Clear plastic rattle wound and cemented on
Eyes Stick on

TUNA FLY

A trolling lure for many pelagic fish. There are also many colour variations.

Hook 6/0 SS O'Shannesy
Tail Silver Mylar tubing
Body Wrapped silver Mylar
Wing White Fishair under blue Fishair
Throat White Fishair
Lateral Flat silver tinsel
Eye Silver tinsel under clear epoxy

WHITE BAIT

Hook 6/0 SS O'Shannesy
Tail Silver Mylar tubing
Body Wrapped silver Mylar
Wing White Fishair
Throat White Fishair
Lateral Flat silver tinsel
Eye Silver tinsel under clear epoxy

SURF BLUE BAIT

The biggest flathead I have heard of in Port Philip was taken on this fly, which was fished as a dropper above a bait. It was a massive 19lb (8.6kg.)

Hook 2/0 SS O'Shannesy
Tail Silver tinsel strands
Body Wrapped silver Mylar tube
Wing White under blue Fishair with silver Crystal Flash
Eye Stick on silver under 2 part epoxy

GREEN SURF FLY

I have memories of a guy I know from the Melbourne boat shows. I know him only as Paul (the tackle rat), sorry Paul. He bought one of these flies at a boat show one Friday. Saturday morning as the show opened here comes Paul running down the hall at the old Melbourne Exhibition Building. He had been surf fishing at dawn. Taken a lot of salmon on this fly and then lost it so had to have more very urgently.

Hook	2/0 SS O'Shannesy
Tail	Silver tinsel
Body	Wrapped green Mylar tube
Wing	Pale grizzle back to back under green Fishair and multi coloured crystal flash
Eyes	Silver stick on under 2 part epoxy

CLOUSER MINNOW

A favourite of late American fly angler Lefty Kreh. There are a great many variations to this fly.

Hook	2/0 SS O'Shannesy
Wing	Fishair with pearl crystal flash
Eyes	Silver bead chain

REFERENCES

An illustrated Dictionary of Trout Flies — **John Roberts**
Published in London in1995 by Collins Willow.

Australia's Best Trout Flies — **Malcom Crosse and Robert Sloane**
Published in Hobart in 1997 by FlyLife Publishing.

Australian Trout Food, Trout Flies and how to fish them — **Rob Flower**
Published in Bayswater Vic. in 2001 by Australian Fishing Network.

Australian Fly Patterns — **Peter Coulson**
Published in 2004 by The Australian Fishing Network.

Caddis Flies — **Gary La Fontaine**
Published in 1989 by Lyons Press in USA.

Czech Nymph and Other Related Fly Fishing Methods — **Karel Krivanec**
Published in 2007 Branisovska, Czech Republic by Grayling and Trout Publishing.

Essential Fly Fishing Techniques — **Neil Grose**
Published in Launceston in 2001 by Fly Guide.

Flies The best 1000 — **Randle Scott Stetzer**
Published in 1992 in Portland Oregon by Frank Amato Publications.

Flies for Trout — Dick Stewart and Farrow Allen
Published in 1993 in North Conway USA by Mountain Pond Publishing

Fly Fisher's Pattern Book — Gene Kugach
Published in 2000 in Mechanicsburg PA by Stackpole Books.

Fly Patterns Collected from 1988 — Rob Flower
Unpublished.

Fly Patterns - an International Guide — Taff Price
Published in 1986 in London by Ward Loch.

Freshwater Fishing Magazine #100 — AFN
Published in Bayswater Vic by Freshwater Fishing.

Further Guide to Fly Dressing — John Veniard
Published in 1965 in London by A. & C. Black.

Modern Trout Flies and how to tie them — Poul Jorgensen
Published in 1979 in London by Ernest Benn Ltd.

Nymph Fishing for Larger Trout — Charles E Brooks
Published in 1976 by Crown Publishers N.Y.

In Pursuit of Fly Tying — George Rowney
Published in 1987 in Melbourne by George Rowney.

Ripples, Runs and Rises — David Scholes
Published in 1988 in Kenthurst NSW by Kangaroo Press.

Tasmanian Trout Flies — Max Stokes
Published in Hobart in 1978 by Cat and fiddle Press.

The Fly Tyer's Companion — Mike Dawes
Published in 1989 in Auckland NZ. by Johnston Co-editions and Mike Dawes

The Lure of Fly Tying — F.A.D.G. Griffiths
Published in 1978 by Murray Book Distributors Ultimo NSW.

The Shannon Rise — R.H. Wigram
Undated, published by Telegraph Printery Pty Ltd Hobart Tas.

Time of the Take — Fred Dunford
Published in 2012 by Tight Lines Press

Trout and Salmon Flies of Wales — Moc Morgan
Published in 1996 by Merlin Unwin Books of Ludlow Shropshire.

Trout Flies for Australia — Maury Wilson
Unpublished

Trout Flies in New Zealand — Keith Draper
Published in 1971 by Heinemann reed of Auckland NZ.

The Sotheby's Guide to Fly-Fishing for Trout — Charles Jardine
Published in 1991 by Dorling Kindersley Ltd London

Trout on a Fly — Lance Wedlick
Undated, Printed by Hedges and Bell Maryborough Vic.

Trout Stream flies in New Zealand — Norman Marsh
Published in 1983 by Millwood Press Ltd Auckland NZ.

World's Best Trout Flies — John Roberts
Published in 1995 by Tiger Books International PLC Twickenham UK.

FLY PATTERNS AND REFERENCE NUMBERS